THE PUZZLE FILES OF LARRY LOGIC

Dan Katz

PUZZLE
WRIGHT
PRESS

New York

PUZZLE
WRIGHT
PRESS
New York

An Imprint of Sterling Publishing Co., Inc.

PUZZLEWRIGHT PRESS and the distinctive Puzzlewright Press logo
are registered trademarks of Sterling Publishing Co., Inc.

This edition published in 2023
Text © 2014 Dan Katz

ISBN 978-1-4549-4929-9

For information about custom editions, special sales, and premium purchases,
please contact specialsales@unionsquareandco.com.

Manufactured in Malaysia

2   4   6   8   10   9   7   5   3   1

unionsquareandco.com

Cover and chapter introduction illustrations © 2023 Giulia Ghigini
Stationery illustrations (pp. 5, 75, 76, 77) © Shutterstock.com/AllNikArt
Thumbprint illustration (p. 78) © Shutterstock.com/lestyan
Cover design by Igor Satanowsky

CONTENTS

INTRODUCTION

I wish I could remember exactly when I first started solving logic problems. I know that in grade school I encountered them as an exercise given to some of the "gifted" students, and also in the various puzzle magazines I begged my parents to buy me at the grocery store. I'm not sure which of those served as my first point of contact, but either way I was hooked early, and I spent a great deal of my young life filling dots and X's into grids.

Although I was nuts for them in my younger years, as I broadened my puzzle horizons over time, I found that traditional logic problems didn't keep me quite as engaged as they used to. Maybe it was the fact that I had solved so many of them, and they were often very similar, seeming to blend together over time. Or maybe it was that I was gravitating toward "aha!" puzzles, puzzles with more of a punchline than just a filled grid. After all, I could figure out that it was Mr. Miller who owned the zebra and not the plumber in the house next door, but unless I was conducting a pet census, did it really matter?

In writing this particular book of logic puzzles, I've tried to "ennui-proof" the puzzles in two ways. First, you'll find that while the puzzles are all solvable by logical deduction, their structures vary from chapter to chapter. You'll be faced with ingredients that are used more than once, trains that aren't used at all, and clues that may or may not be accurate; you'll need to reconstruct vault combinations, rendezvous schedules, and suspects' positions on a grid. Make sure you read the instructions at the beginning of each chapter, so you know the rules for that particular set of puzzles.

Second, I wanted the puzzles to have more of an objective than simply figuring out who did what where. So each chapter is accompanied by a story set in Enigmaville, the home of puzzle-solving policeman Lieutenant Larry Logic. In order to solve the latest crime, you'll need to work out five logic puzzles, and then use the answers to those puzzles to solve a sixth, final puzzle. To top it off, the answers to those ten final puzzles will help you solve one additional puzzle, the ultimate objective of the book. If you're like me and enjoy working toward a meaningful goal, that's a pretty strongly defined one.

Whether you're still excited by standard logic problems, or you're already looking for something a little different, I hope you'll find the puzzles in this book stimulating and satisfying. And once you've conquered all of the interconnected conundrums, you may not know who owns the zebra, but you'll know the name of Enigmaville's most diabolical criminal mastermind. If you'd like to picture your nemesis with a pet zebra in his or her lap, that's totally up to you.

—Dan Katz

WELCOME TO ENIGMAVILLE!

There are eight million stories in the naked city … but this is Enigmaville, and we wear clothes here, thank you very much. I haven't taken the time to count all the stories that go down in this little burg, but I can tell you for sure there are at least ten; what's more, I can share them with you, and hopefully you can help me and my squad out with the endings.

But I'm getting ahead of myself. My name's Larry Logic, Lieutenant Larry Logic of the Enigmaville P.D. Before you ask, the last name's legit; my dad was Leonard Logic, and his dad was Luther Logic. It's a pretty big coincidence, though, because here's the thing about Enigmaville. In your average town, when somebody commits a crime, you have to scour the scene for evidence, catch your perp in a lie, and basically reinvent the wheel every time you want to punish a lowlife for taking advantage of innocent people. For some reason, that's not the way things go here. In Enigmaville, there's never enough information at hand to know immediately what happened, but somehow there's always enough to work things out through logical deduction. It's kind of crazy, but I try to accept it without asking too many questions.

I've become kind of a department celebrity, since my logic skills are second to none, so I'm the go-to guy when the weird recon starts rolling in. Used to be we'd get one or two tough cases a month, I'd furrow my brow for a few hours, and things would be sorted out. Recently, though, we've been swamped. It seems every criminal in the metropolitan area is making their move at the same time. With this kind of volume, I'm going to need some help. So I'm bringing you ten cases, and I'm hoping you'll bring me some assistance. For each case, you'll find five separate situations that need to be sorted out independently; once you've solved those five, the information you've generated should be all you need to put the last part of the case to bed.

Now that I think about it, it's hard to imagine that the local crime rate would increase this steeply without there being more to it. Makes you wonder whether there's some kind of criminal overlord pulling the strings. But I guess there's really no way to know, unless he decides to make his presence known. Until then, best of luck, and thanks for the help. You're providing a great service to the people of Enigmaville.

Deductively yours,
Lieutenant Larry Logic

THE CASE OF THE SUBSTANDARD SUBSTITUTE

You know how some people say, "Those who can, do; those who can't, teach"? I can tell you from personal experience that's a load of malarkey. It ought to be "Those who can't teach, do; those who can teach, teach." Let me tell you a little story to explain what I mean. Last year on Take Your Kid to Work Day, I took it upon myself to try to show the precinct tykes how to take fingerprints. How hard could it be to teach them something we do every day? After the first five minutes, frankly everything's a blur, but it took us more than two weeks to get all the ink off the refrigerator.

So I've got nothing but respect for America's educators and what they go through to train for what they do. And it fries my bacon when somebody walks in off the street thinking they can do the same job, especially when that joker should really be behind bars. But I'm getting ahead of myself.

A felon who goes by the name "the Phantom," a malevolent master of disguise, recently sprung himself loose from a prison not too far from Enigmaville. Authorities trailed the Phantom here, and word on the street is he's been impersonating a substitute teacher at a local high school all week. Unfortunately, the Phantom is so adept at changing his appearance that we could look him straight in the eye and not know for sure it was him. He's even passed for a woman in the past, so any sub is a suspect, male or female.

So we carted in every substitute teacher from Enigmaville's five major high schools for questioning. Hopefully if we grill them effectively enough, we can figure out which ones are legit instructors, and which one is just pretending to profess.

Instructions: For each puzzle, determine the first and last names of each substitute teacher, the subject they taught, and the high school at which they taught. In each suspect group, every teacher taught a different subject, and they each taught at a different school. The subjects covered are history, literature, math, science, and Spanish; and the schools are Coolidge, Kennedy, Polk, Roosevelt, and Garfield. However, not every subject and every school is used in every puzzle (any unused schools are specified in Clue 1).

Solutions for this chapter are on pages 79–80.

SUSPECT GROUP 1

1. The three suspects in Group 1 had the first names Bert, Bob, and Byron, and their last names were Bell, Bradley, and Bundy. None of them taught literature or Spanish, and none of them taught at Coolidge or Roosevelt.

2. Bert and the math teacher were brought in ten minutes before the teacher from Kennedy High School arrived.

3. Byron taught at Garfield, while the history teacher taught at Polk.

4. Mr. Bradley, who didn't teach math, seemed slightly uncomfortable around Bob Bundy.

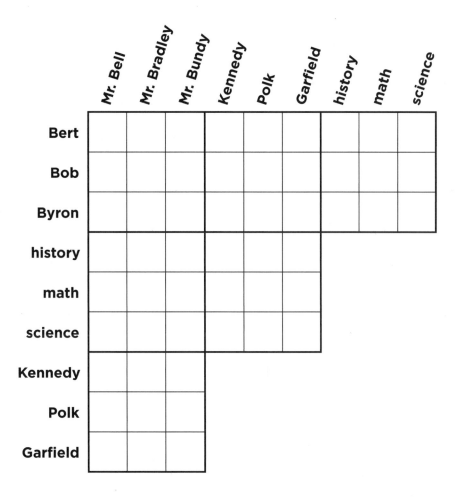

SUSPECT GROUP 2

1.   The first names of the suspects in Group 2 were Daria, Delia, Diana, and Dolores; their last names were Dedham, Dickson, Dryden, and Dunn. None of these four taught math or taught at Garfield.

2.   The sub at Kennedy High taught Spanish, whereas Diana Dunn taught at a different school.

3.   The teachers at Polk and Roosevelt were (in some order) Ms. Dickson and the history teacher (who wasn't named Daria or Dolores).

4.   Delia taught at either Coolidge or Roosevelt.

5.   Daria and the teacher from Coolidge High School both claimed to have been teaching for at least five years. In contrast, Ms. Dryden and the literature teacher said they recently earned their teaching licenses.

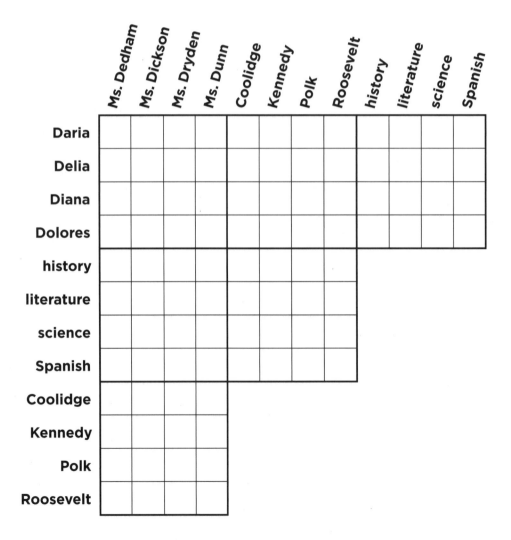

SUSPECT GROUP 3

1. The four suspects in Group 3 had the first names Harriet, Helen, Hester, and Hilda, and the last names Hall, Harris, Hayes, and Hubbard. None of them taught science, and none taught at Polk High School.

2. Neither Ms. Harris nor Ms. Hall (the teacher at Roosevelt) taught history, and neither of them were named Helen.

3. Ms. Hubbard and the teacher from Kennedy, who were in some order the literature and Spanish teachers, passed the time at the police department with an enthusiastic discussion about El Cid. Harriet and the teacher from Garfield High did not participate.

4. Hester Hayes was mildly jealous of the expensive clothes worn by Hilda, who was not the literature teacher.

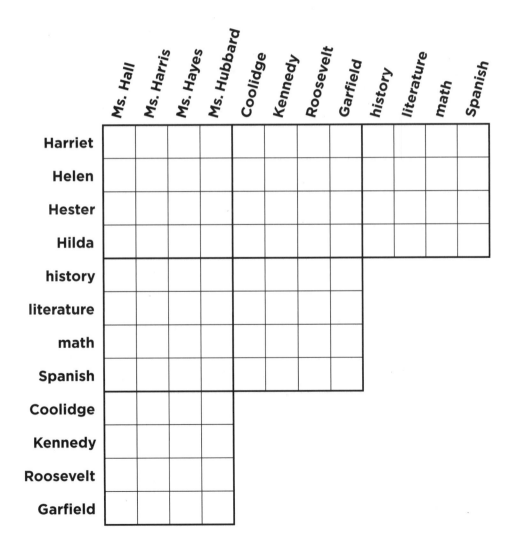

SUSPECT GROUP 4

1. Group 4 consisted of suspects named Jacqueline, Jessica, Jill, Joan, and Julie, with the last names James, Jeffries, Jenkins, Johnston, and Jordan. All subjects and schools were represented.

2. Jill and the Spanish teacher were, in some order, Ms. Jenkins (who was not named Jacqueline) and Ms. Jordan (who taught at either Polk or Roosevelt).

3. The teacher from Coolidge High School taught either history or Spanish.

4. Jessica felt her math class went much better than the class Joan taught at Roosevelt.

5. The literature teacher and the teacher who subbed at Kennedy were, in some order, Ms. Jeffries (who was named either Jacqueline or Julie) and Ms. James.

6. Ms. Johnston taught at Garfield High School, while the science teacher was busy subbing at Polk High.

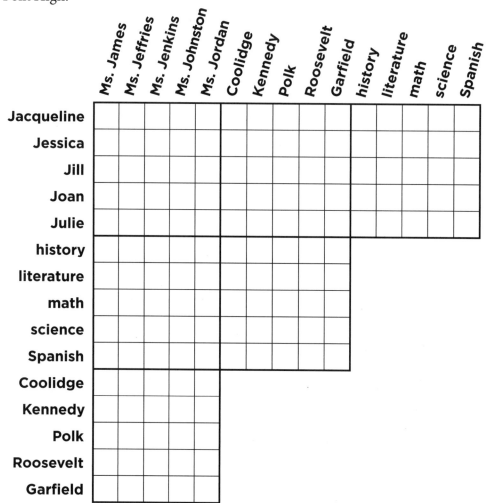

SUSPECT GROUP 5

1. The first names of the suspects in Group 5 were Ralph, Ray, Reggie, Roland, and Ryan, and the last names were Randall, Redding, Richards, Roberts, and Ruiz. The suspects taught all five subjects at all five schools.

2. Roland, Mr. Ruiz, and the teacher from Garfield High sat in three different corners of the room while they waited to be questioned.

3. Ray, Reggie (who didn't teach literature or Spanish), and Roland were (in some order) the history teacher, Mr. Roberts (who didn't teach at Coolidge), and the teacher from Roosevelt.

4. The students at Polk High School seemed to really enjoy their class with Mr. Richards.

5. Ralph taught neither the science class nor the math class (which was taught by Mr. Randall).

6. The teacher who subbed at Kennedy High taught literature.

7. Mr. Redding and the teacher from Garfield's first names are Ralph and Ryan, in some order.

8. The science teacher wasn't Reggie and didn't teach at Coolidge High.

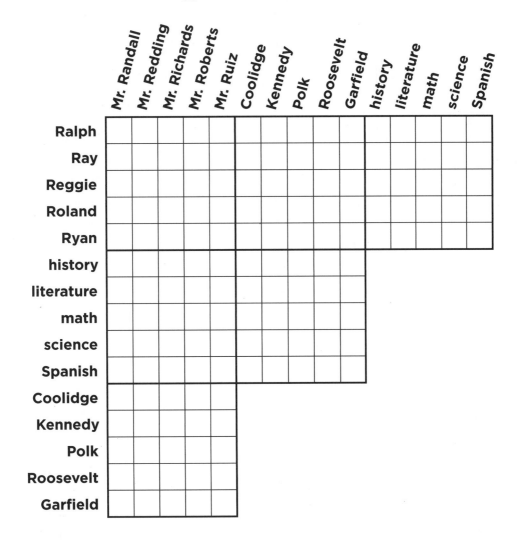

After some in-depth investigation, we are fairly confident that the impostor is one of seven alleged substitutes: Mr. Bradley, Ms. Dryden, Ms. Harris, Ms. James, Ms. Jenkins, Mr. Roberts, and Mr. Ruiz. After questioning, the seven remaining suspects were allowed to leave, but we kept a close eye on them. Six of the suspects split into pairs and went out for drinks, engaging in pretty convincing conversations about their respective teaching experiences. The seventh is most likely the Phantom.

Unfortunately, the rookie we sent to tail them delivered a fairly cryptic report. Nonetheless, from the information below, it should be possible to determine which three pairs of teachers got chummy, and who was the odd one out.

1. No pair of teachers that went out together taught at the same school.

2. Two teachers that taught the same subject went out separately, one with a teacher who taught at Polk, and one with a teacher who taught at Kennedy.

3. The teacher who went out alone didn't teach science.

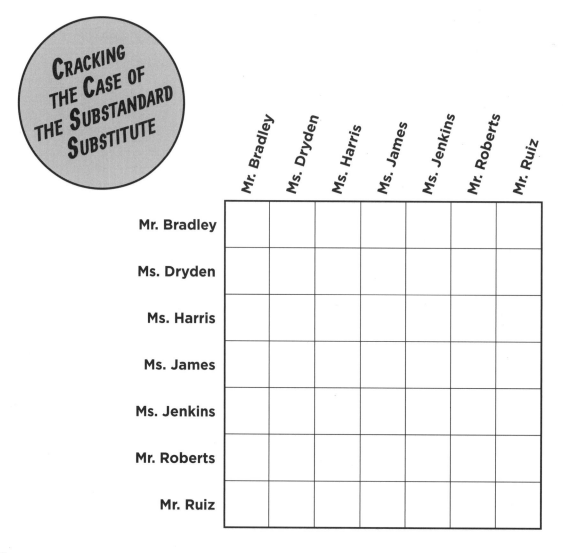

THE CASE OF THE TRUE LEBLEU

As the old saying goes, I don't know art, but I know what I like … and I know I don't like art. And I especially don't like the art of Pierre LeBleu, the hip modern artist who specializes in "experimental explorations of variations on the color blue." That's how Pierre describes his work; personally, I'd describe it as a bunch of solid blue canvases that look identical yet sell for millions of euros.

Since it's pretty easy to throw a bucket of blue paint at an easel, there's a thriving market of imitation LeBleu paintings for the pretentious hipster who wants a conversation piece without taking out a second mortgage. These faux LeBleus draw a lot of attention, but even I was surprised last month when five consecutive auctions at five different Enigmaville auction houses each saw an imitation sell for at least a thousand bucks. To make things smell fishier, the same buyers seemed to be turning up over and over again.

I started to connect the dots when I heard about a big robbery at a nearby art museum. A few dozen paintings were lifted, and most of them have since been recovered on the black market. But there's still one hot LeBleu piece that hasn't turned up, and unless I miss my guess, it was sold at one of these auctions. That means one of these five buyers is actually holding on to a big blue rectangle worth millions; the other four were probably accomplices, hired to buy up fakes and draw attention away from the real McCoy.

The buyers kept low profiles, replacing their real names with colorful aliases. (As long as the buyer pays in cash, auctioneers don't ask too many questions.) I've got my feelers out trying to figure out as much information as possible about which of the paintings was actually legit, but I'm pretty sure that first we're going to need to know which buyer spent what at each of the auctions. Then we can track down the stolen goods.

Instructions: For each puzzle, determine which of the five auction houses (Agatha's, Beverly's, Clarissa's, Darlene's, or Eloise's) sold a supposedly imitation LeBleu to each buyer (Mr. Black, Mr. Brown, Mr. Gold, Mr. Green, or Mr. White), and for which price ($1000, $2000, $3000, $4000, or $5000). In two of the puzzles, you'll also need to determine the paintings' genres.

Solutions for this chapter are on pages 80–81.

Auction Week 1

1. The painting at Clarissa's sold for $1000.

2. Mr. Black and the buyer at Agatha's spent a total of $7000.

3. Mr. Green, the $3000 buyer, and the buyer at Eloise's each arrived to their auctions on time; in contrast, the buyer that spent $2000 and the buyer at Beverly's showed up late.

4. Mr. Brown was pleased to get his painting for $4000.

5. If you add the cost of Mr. Gold's painting to the cost of the painting purchased at Eloise's, the result is a multiple of $3000.

	Mr. Black	Mr. Brown	Mr. Gold	Mr. Green	Mr. White	$1000	$2000	$3000	$4000	$5000
Agatha's										
Beverly's										
Clarissa's										
Darlene's										
Eloise's										
$1000										
$2000										
$3000										
$4000										
$5000										

Auction Week 2

1. Mr. Brown paid $2000 more for his painting than the buyer at Clarissa's did for his.

2. Mr. Black and the buyer at Darlene's spent $2000 and $5000 on their paintings (in some order). Mr. Gold and the Agatha's buyer spent $1000 and $3000 (in some order).

3. One buyer (not Mr. White) spent $1000 more than the buyer at Eloise's.

4. Mr. Green's painting cost twice as much as the painting purchased at Beverly's.

	Mr. Black	Mr. Brown	Mr. Gold	Mr. Green	Mr. White	$1000	$2000	$3000	$4000	$5000
Agatha's										
Beverly's										
Clarissa's										
Darlene's										
Eloise's										
$1000										
$2000										
$3000										
$4000										
$5000										

Auction Week 3

1. The total cost of the painting sold at Agatha's and the painting sold to Mr. Gold was at least $6000.

2. The painting sold at Beverly's cost $3000 less than another painting; that second painting wasn't purchased by Mr. Green.

3. Mr. Brown, who didn't buy his painting at Agatha's, spent exactly as much as Mr. White and the Darlene's buyer combined.

4. The total cost of the paintings bought by Mr. Green and Mr. Black was $4000 more than the total cost of the paintings from Beverly's and Clarissa's. (These were four different paintings.)

	Mr. Black	Mr. Brown	Mr. Gold	Mr. Green	Mr. White	$1000	$2000	$3000	$4000	$5000
Agatha's										
Beverly's										
Clarissa's										
Darlene's										
Eloise's										
$1000					
$2000					
$3000					
$4000					
$5000					

AUCTION WEEK 4

1. The five paintings sold this week were advertised as five different types: a landscape, a mural, a portrait, a seascape, and a still life. (This was in spite of the fact that they were all just blue.)

2. The painting sold at Beverly's and the painting sold to Mr. Gold cost a total of $5000.

3. The portrait sold at Agatha's cost $1000 more than the painting bought from Clarissa's, and $2000 less than the painting bought by Mr. Green.

4. The still life, the painting from Darlene's, and Mr. White's painting were three different paintings.

5. Mr. Brown bought the mural at half the cost of the seascape sold at Eloise's.

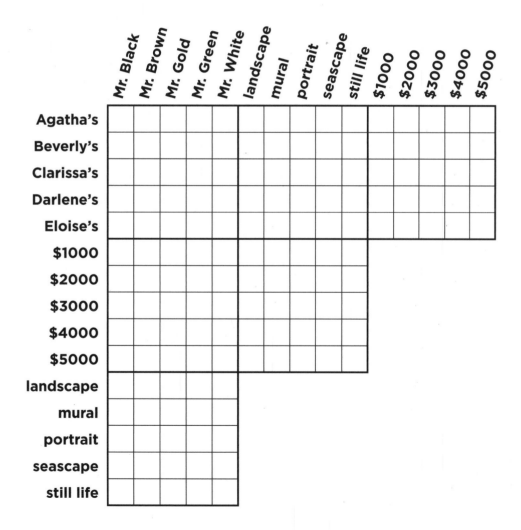

Auction Week 5

1. The five paintings sold were again all of different types (the same types as in the previous week's auctions).

2. The painting sold at Eloise's was less expensive than the still life, which was less expensive than the landscape.

3. The seascape was more expensive than the painting sold at Darlene's, which was more expensive than the painting bought by Mr. Gold.

4. Beverly's sold a painting for $2000 more than Mr. Green spent.

5. Mr. Black (who did not buy the seascape) and Mr. White saw each other at an Italian restaurant before the auctions; meanwhile, the buyers who made purchases at Beverly's and Clarissa's went for tacos. The fifth buyer, who bought the mural, skipped dinner.

6. The portrait was sold for $4000.

7. Mr. Green was not the buyer at Eloise's, and he did not buy a painting for $3000.

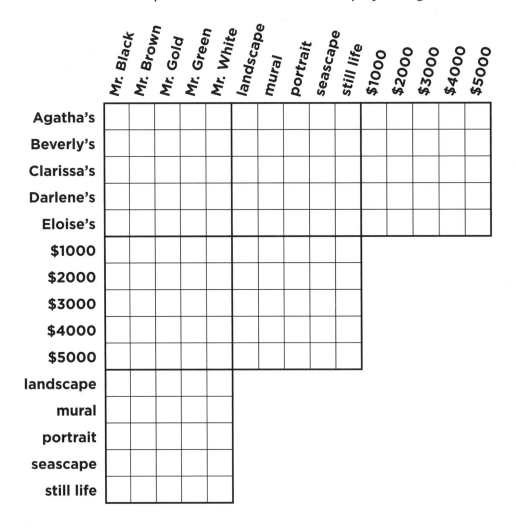

As it turns out, the five buyers have been identified as David Chartreuse, William Puce, John Turquoise, Richard Umber, and Arthur Vermilion. Unfortunately, we're still not sure which buyer used which pseudonym. The information below should help you figure out which buyer used which identity, and specifically which of the twenty-five paintings is the stolen one.

1. Neither Arthur Vermilion nor William Puce bought paintings from four different auction houses.

2. One auction house sold four paintings for the same price. The one painting that this auction house sold at a different price went to either William Puce or John Turquoise.

3. Arthur Vermilion spent $2000 more than Richard Umber. At least one of Vermilion's paintings was bought for a price Umber never spent on any painting.

4. After the last two weeks of auctions, two buyers ended up with a pair of paintings in the same two genres. The week the stolen painting was purchased, together these two buyers spent exactly double the cost of the stolen painting.

5. One of the buyers spent exactly $1000 more than David Chartreuse on two occasions; this buyer did not buy the stolen painting.

CRACKING THE CASE OF THE TRUE LeBleu

	Mr. Black	Mr. Brown	Mr. Gold	Mr. Green	Mr. White
David Chartreuse					
William Puce					
John Turquoise					
Richard Umber					
Arthur Vermilion					

THE CASE OF THE UNKNOWN CALZONE

As much as I thrive on investigating on my own, sometimes you need a little help from your friends. And when I do, I can usually count on a private investigator friend of mine, Tyson "Sure" Locke. People call him "Sure" for two reasons: they get a kick out of the detective pun, and Sure never says no to any mystery. Even if it's a case that could get him into trouble.

Unfortunately, that's just what happened recently, when he started looking into a string of disappearances that led him to Itty-Bitty Italy. Itty-Bitty Italy's one of the rougher neighborhoods in Enigmaville; it's a great place to go if you want a good cannoli, a well-tailored suit, or the opportunity to never be heard from again. I've been trying to reach Sure for some time, and he's not answering his phone; I have a feeling that while trailing the kidnappers, Sure became a kidnappee.

I hacked into Sure's notes and followed his trail, and it looks like he uncovered a pretty major conspiracy centered around Mario's Calzones on Liberty Street. It's not a particularly busy restaurant, but it's a lot more popular among people associated with the kidnapping ring; Sure's theory is they're sending coded messages based on the types of calzones they serve to their "special" customers. If we're going to intercept any of these communications, we'll need to figure out their code, and the first step to doing that is figuring out what's been served during their last five lunches.

Instructions: For each puzzle, determine the ingredients in the calzone served at each table. Within each puzzle, every calzone has the same number of ingredients, although no two calzones in the same puzzle have the exact same set of ingredients. Also, within each puzzle, every ingredient occurs the same number of times.

Solutions for this chapter are on pages 82–83.

LUNCH 1

1. Four tables each received a two-ingredient calzone. The ingredients were meatballs, onions, peppers, and sausage.

2. Tables 3 and 4 had one ingredient in common, but it wasn't meatballs. Tables 2 and 3 had one ingredient in common, but it wasn't onions.

3. Together, tables 1 and 3 had all four ingredients.

4. Table 2 had sausage. Table 4 didn't have onions.

	Ingredient 1	Ingredient 2
Table 1		
Table 2		
Table 3		
Table 4		

INGREDIENTS:

meatballs
onions
peppers
sausage

LUNCH 2

1. Five tables each received a two-ingredient calzone. The ingredients were basil, chicken, ham, pepperoni, and sausage.

2. Table 5 didn't have chicken or ham.

3. Table 1 had basil, while tables 2 and 4 together had every ingredient except sausage.

4. Tables 2 and 3 had one ingredient in common; tables 3 and 5 also had an ingredient in common, which wasn't pepperoni.

5. No table had both basil and ham.

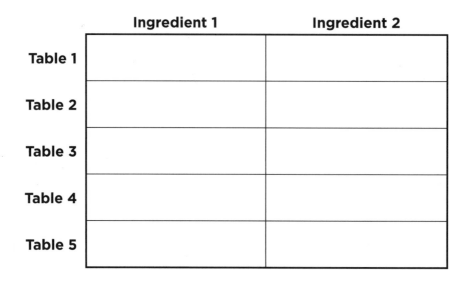

	Ingredient 1	Ingredient 2
Table 1		
Table 2		
Table 3		
Table 4		
Table 5		

INGREDIENTS:

basil

chicken

ham

pepperoni

sausage

LUNCH 3

1. Six tables each received a two-ingredient calzone. The ingredients were bacon, chicken, ham, meatballs, peppers, and spinach.

2. Tables 3 and 5 had one ingredient in common, but it wasn't bacon. Tables 3 and 4 didn't have any ingredients in common.

3. Table 2 had a calzone with ham in it, and table 6 had chicken.

4. There were no peppers at table 3 or 6, and there was no ham at table 4. The table 1 calzone did include spinach.

5. Among the calzones at tables 2, 3, and 5, exactly one of them had chicken.

6. Tables 1, 4, and 5 had all six ingredients between them.

	Ingredient 1	Ingredient 2
Table 1		
Table 2		
Table 3		
Table 4		
Table 5		
Table 6		

INGREDIENTS:

bacon

chicken

ham

meatballs

peppers

spinach

LUNCH 4

1. Five tables each received a three-ingredient calzone. The ingredients were basil, chicken, onions, peppers, and sausage.

2. Table 3's calzone included sausage, and Table 4's contained onions.

3. Tables 1 and 4 had exactly one ingredient in common, whereas tables 2 and 5 had two in common.

4. Table 2 had a calzone with peppers, and table 5 had a chicken calzone.

5. Only one table had both chicken and basil. Also, only one table (not table 2 or 3) had both sausage and peppers.

6. Table 1 had basil, but not sausage.

	Ingredient 1	Ingredient 2	Ingredient 3
Table 1			
Table 2			
Table 3			
Table 4			
Table 5			

INGREDIENTS:

basil

chicken

onions

peppers

sausage

LUNCH 5

1. Six tables each received a three-ingredient calzone. The ingredients were bacon, basil, meatballs, onions, pepperoni, and spinach.

2. Tables 1 and 5 had no ingredients in common. Tables 4 and 6 had two ingredients in common. Tables 2 and 6 had at least one ingredient in common.

3. The table 3 calzone contained basil, but neither spinach nor meatballs.

4. There were exactly two onion calzones among the calzones at tables 4, 5, and 6.

5. Table 1 had bacon, while table 2 had meatballs. There was no pepperoni in the calzone at table 5, nor was there basil at table 2.

	Ingredient 1	Ingredient 2	Ingredient 3
Table 1			
Table 2			
Table 3			
Table 4			
Table 5			
Table 6			

INGREDIENTS:

bacon

basil

meatballs

onions

pepperoni

spinach

This morning there was good news and bad news. The good news is that this morning, the kidnapping ring, headed up by bitter restaurateur Mario Desmond, was busted, as the feds came in and did what they do best. The bad news is that Sure Locke is nowhere to be found; it seems like the kidnappers shipped him out of town, and we have no idea where to start looking. It's not likely that they managed to smuggle him out of the country, but that doesn't narrow things down much.

The only trace is a delicious calzone with his name on it. I don't mean one he was going to eat; it actually has his name written on it in tomato paste. Now that we have the run of the place, there's a lot of info available about how the coded transmissions work at Mario's. Hopefully we can crack the code and figure out what United States location is being signaled by the Sure Locke calzone.

1. Each calzone ingredient represented a different digit from 0 to 9. If you oriented the thickest part of the calzone down, the ingredients were arranged from left to right; thus, each calzone translated to a multi-digit number. (Too bad we don't know anything about the order of ingredients in the earlier calzones.)

2. A "36" calzone was served at the lunch immediately before a lunch with a "53" calzone.

3. A "568" calzone was served at the lunch immediately before a lunch with an "801" calzone.

4. There was never a "48" or "84" calzone served, but there was a "47" calzone at one of the lunches.

5. One of the calzones at Lunch 3 translated to "12."

6. The Sure Locke calzone contains, in order, spinach, bacon, onions, sausage, and ham.

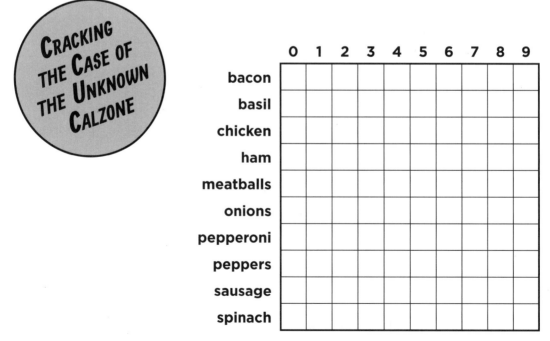

THE CASE OF THE SINFUL CINEPHILES

There's a saying in Enigmaville: "Show me what you do in the dark, and I'll show you who you truly are." It's the kind of saying that suggests we have some issues when it comes to privacy, but it also means I probably should have been less surprised when we heard there was trouble at the Enigmaville Multiplex. After all, if you're looking to get away with something in the dark, there aren't a lot of other public places where they officially kill the lights multiple times a day. Apparently a gang of smugglers is using the movie theater as a crime scene, passing off illegal narcotics after the opening credits roll. And I thought that stuff they put on the popcorn was addictive.

We brought in eight suspects who each saw multiple showings of the same movie in the same week. In any other month, that kind of suspicious behavior would be a major red flag. Unfortunately, *Galactic Conflict VII* just hit theaters, and the nerd contingent is out in full force. The multiplex is showing this movie three times a night, and it's not clear which of our suspects are returning to exchange ill-gotten gains, and which are just devoted Galackies who want to repeatedly watch the scene where Commander Glarf shockingly betrays his longtime protégé. I mean, how could he do that? They fought in the Jupiter War together! It's enough to … ahem. Sorry. Back to the matter at hand.

GC VII is showing three times a night, at 6 P.M., 9 P.M., and midnight. We know each suspect was in the vicinity of the multiplex twice throughout the week, and our first order of business is figuring out who went to which showings on which night. Once we have that information, we can use our investigative work to figure out who's handing off contraband under cover of sci-fi, and who's guilty of nothing more than a love of interplanetary drama.

Instructions: For each puzzle, determine which of the three showings (6 P.M., 9 P.M., and midnight) each of the given suspects attended. Each suspect may have attended any combination of the three showings (including none at all), but within any puzzle, no two suspects attended exactly the same combination of showings.

Solutions for this chapter are on pages 83–85.

27

MONDAY NIGHT

Steve, Trixie, Ursula, and Valerie are known to have been near the theater on Monday.

1. Either Trixie attended the 9 P.M. showing and Ursula attended the 6 P.M. showing, or neither of these events occurred.

2. Either Steve attended the 6 P.M. showing and Ursula attended the midnight showing, or neither of these events occurred.

3. Either Valerie attended the midnight showing and Steve attended the 9 P.M. showing, or neither of these events occurred.

4. Steve, Trixie, and Valerie each attended exactly two showings. No suspect attended all three.

5. Steve and Valerie were not both present at the midnight showing.

	6 P.M.	9 P.M.	midnight
Steve			
Trixie			
Ursula			
Valerie			

TUESDAY NIGHT

Walter, Xavier, Yvette, and Ziggy are known to have been near the theater on Tuesday.

1. Xavier attended the 6 P.M. showing, and Walter attended the midnight showing.

2. Exactly two out of three of the following events occurred: Walter attended the 9 P.M. showing; Yvette attended the midnight showing; Ziggy attended the 6 P.M. showing.

3. Exactly two out of three of the following events occurred: Xavier attended the midnight showing; Yvette attended the 9 P.M. showing; Ziggy attended the 6 P.M. showing.

4. More of the suspects attended the midnight showing than the 6 P.M. showing. Exactly three suspects were at the 9 P.M. showing.

5. Ziggy attended more showings than Xavier did.

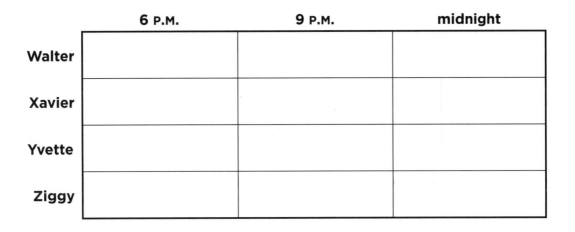

	6 P.M.	9 P.M.	midnight
Walter			
Xavier			
Yvette			
Ziggy			

Wednesday Night

Steve, Valerie, Walter, Yvette, and Ziggy are known to have been near the theater on Wednesday.

1. Either Walter and Yvette both attended the midnight showing, or neither of them did.

2. Valerie attended more showings than Ziggy did.

3. Every showing was attended by either two or three suspects. Steve was not one of the suspects at the 9 P.M. showing.

4. Walter attended the 6 P.M. showing, and Ziggy attended the midnight showing.

5. No suspect attended both the 6 P.M. and 9 P.M. showings.

	6 P.M.	9 P.M.	midnight
Steve			
Valerie			
Walter			
Yvette			
Ziggy			

THURSDAY NIGHT

Steve, Trixie, Ursula, Walter, and Xavier are known to have been near the theater on Thursday.

1. Either Walter and Trixie both attended the 9 P.M. showing, or neither of them did. At least one of Trixie and Xavier was at the 6 P.M. showing.

2. No one attended all three showings or missed all three showings.

3. The number of showings attended by Steve was the same as the number of suspects attending the midnight showing.

4. Either Ursula attended the 6 P.M. showing and Xavier attended the 9 P.M. showing, or neither of these events occurred.

5. The number of showings attended by Ursula was the same as the number of suspects attending the 6 P.M. showing.

6. Walter attended the midnight showing.

	6 P.M.	9 P.M.	midnight
Steve			
Trixie			
Ursula			
Walter			
Xavier			

FRIDAY NIGHT

Trixie, Ursula, Valerie, Xavier, Yvette, and Ziggy are known to have been near the theater on Friday.

1. Either Xavier attended the 6 P.M. showing and Ziggy attended the midnight showing, or neither of these events occurred.

2. Either Valerie attended the 6 P.M. showing and Ursula attended the 9 P.M. showing, or neither of these events occurred.

3. Any suspect who attended the midnight showing also attended the 9 P.M. showing.

4. Ziggy attended more showings than Trixie.

5. Yvette attended the 6 P.M. showing, and Trixie attended the 9 P.M. showing.

6. Exactly one of Ursula, Valerie, and Yvette missed the midnight showing.

7. Exactly one of Trixie, Ursula, and Ziggy missed the 6 P.M. showing.

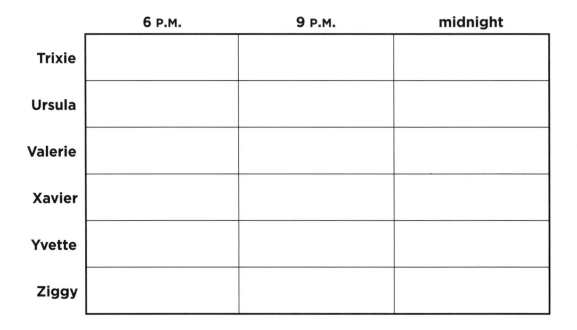

	6 P.M.	9 P.M.	midnight
Trixie			
Ursula			
Valerie			
Xavier			
Yvette			
Ziggy			

Thanks to some diligent investigation, we now know that the gang consists of four smugglers, so half of the suspects we picked up should be guilty. The information below should allow you to help us differentiate the four felons from the four film fanatics.

1. Two of the smugglers attended the same total number of showings. A third smuggler attended fewer, and the fourth attended even fewer.

2. Every smuggler attended at least one midnight showing, but no smuggler attended three.

3. Exactly one smuggler had a night where they were in the area and attended either all three showings or no showings at all. Each of the other six combinations of showings was seen by at least one smuggler on at least one night.

4. Of the smugglers who were in the area on Thursday, at most one of them missed the 9 P.M. showing.

CRACKING THE CASE OF THE SINFUL CINEPHILES

	secretly a smuggler	simply a sci-fi superfan
Steve		
Trixie		
Ursula		
Valerie		
Walter		
Xavier		
Yvette		
Ziggy		

THE CASE OF THE ACROBATIC ARCHBANDITS

There are two sides to every coin, and two sides to every crime-fighting resource. Take informants, for instance; sometimes they're the only thing that can break open a case, and sometimes they're so irritating you want to break open your skull. I can be pretty sure the second one's going to happen any time Curt "Coinflip" Flannigan walks into my office, but I've gotta put up with him because a lot of times he makes the first one happen as well. Coinflip's big issue is a rare personality disorder that causes him to tell a lie every time he tells the truth. Furthermore, these statements don't always come through in that order, so when we get information from him, we have to sort out the true information from the falsehoods.

Coinflip's latest batch of half-reliable scoops concern a sextet of brigand brothers who grew up together in the circus: the Flying Ravioli Brothers. The Raviolis are acrobats by day, but they've been known to break into banks by night. Their unique physical abilities make standard security measures significantly less secure, as they can leap over laser beams and contort their bodies through small spaces. So any time they roll into Enigmaville, there's a good chance trouble is going to follow.

Every spring, Enigmaville hosts a series of gymnastics meets—exhibition events psyching up the athletes and spectators for a state championship later in the year. Apparently the Raviolis showed up to participate in all five meets; Coinflip was there and dug up information on what they did and how well they did it. Not the most important information in the world, but apparently it's tied into Coinflip's notes about their upcoming bank heist, so we'll need to weave our way through his gymnastics reports before we can prevent them from taking home any gold that they didn't win fair and square.

Instructions: In each puzzle, each Ravioli brother competed in a different gymnastics event; determine what event each of them entered, and what score each of them earned. (The score for each event is given for the first two puzzles.)

For each pair of clues (labeled a and b), one of the two statements is true and the other is false. Note that a false clue may incorrectly imply that two descriptions apply to different people when they do not. For example, if the statement "Fabio's score was lower than the score on the rings" is true, Fabio clearly did not compete on the rings; but if this were the false statement, Fabio may or may not have competed on the rings.

Solutions for this chapter are on pages 85–86.

GYMNASTICS MEET 1

The five brothers who competed at this meet (Antonio, Fabio, Giacomo, Luigi, and Marcello) scored 10 on the parallel bars, 9 on the horse, 8 on the rings, 7 in the vault, and 6 on the trampoline … but while the scores are known, it's not clear who participated in which event.

T F

1. ☐ ☐ a) Giacomo competed on the parallel bars.
   ☐ ☐ b) Marcello competed on the horse.

2. ☐ ☐ a) Antonio competed either in the vault or on the rings.
   ☐ ☐ b) Fabio competed on either the trampoline or the horse.

3. ☐ ☐ a) Giacomo competed either in the vault or on the trampoline.
   ☐ ☐ b) Luigi competed on the rings.

4. ☐ ☐ a) Marcello competed on the rings.
   ☐ ☐ b) Antonio competed on the trampoline.

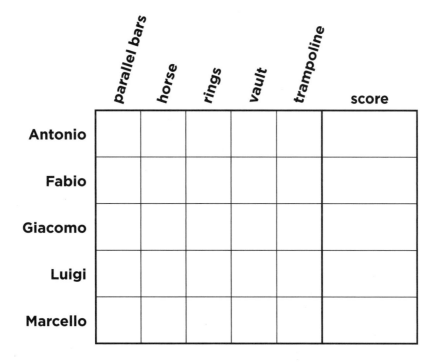

GYMNASTICS MEET 2

All six Ravioli brothers (Antonio, Fabio, Giacomo, Luigi, Marcello, and Primo) participated in this meet; they scored 10 in the floor exercise, 9 on the parallel bars, 8 on the vault, 7 on the horse, 6 on the trampoline, and 5 on the rings.

T F

1. ☐ ☐ a) Marcello competed on the trampoline.
   ☐ ☐ b) Antonio competed in the vault.

2. ☐ ☐ a) Luigi and Primo competed on the horse and trampoline (in some order).
   ☐ ☐ b) Fabio and Giacomo competed on the rings and trampoline (in some order).

3. ☐ ☐ a) Either Fabio or Marcello competed on the rings.
   ☐ ☐ b) Either Fabio or Luigi competed on the horse.

4. ☐ ☐ a) Primo did not compete on the parallel bars.
   ☐ ☐ b) Fabio did not compete in the floor exercise.

5. ☐ ☐ a) Giacomo competed either on the parallel bars or in the floor exercise.
   ☐ ☐ b) Antonio competed either in the floor exercise or on the trampoline.

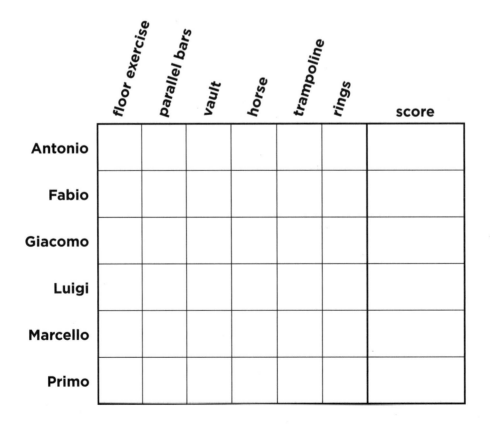

GYMNASTICS MEET 3

Fabio, Luigi, and Primo participated in the third meet, in the horse, trampoline, and floor exercise events. Their scores, in some order, were 10, 9, and 8.

T   F

1. ☐ ☐ a) Fabio competed in the floor exercise.
   ☐ ☐ b) Primo competed on the horse.

2. ☐ ☐ a) Luigi's score was an 8.
   ☐ ☐ b) The score on the trampoline was a 10.

3. ☐ ☐ a) Primo did not score a 9.
   ☐ ☐ b) Luigi did not compete on the horse.

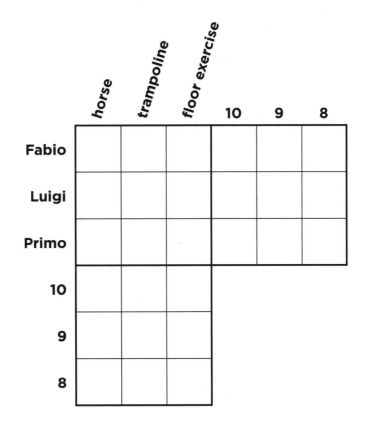

GYMNASTICS MEET 4

Antonio, Giacomo, Marcello, and Primo competed in four different events: the floor exercise, the horse, the parallel bars, and the rings. Their four scores, in some order, were 10, 9, 8, and 7.

T F

1. ☐ ☐ a) Antonio did not compete in the floor exercise.
   ☐ ☐ b) Primo did not compete on the rings.

2. ☐ ☐ a) Giacomo's score was lower than the score on the parallel bars.
   ☐ ☐ b) Marcello's score was higher than 8.

3. ☐ ☐ a) Antonio scored a 9 in his event.
   ☐ ☐ b) Primo did not score an 8 in his event.

4. ☐ ☐ a) Antonio's score was lower than Giacomo's score.
   ☐ ☐ b) Giacomo's score was lower than Primo's score.

5. ☐ ☐ a) One brother scored a 9 on the rings.
   ☐ ☐ b) Primo's score was a 7.

6. ☐ ☐ a) Marcello's score was a 9.
   ☐ ☐ b) Giacomo scored a 10 in his event.

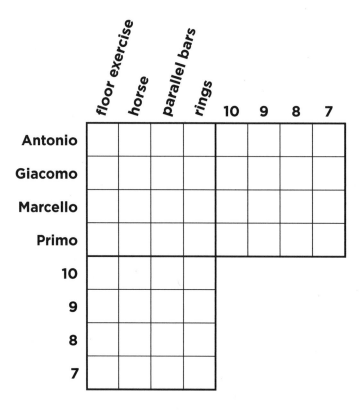

38

GYMNASTICS MEET 5

Five brothers competed in this meet: Antonio, Fabio, Giacomo, Marcello, and Primo. The events they competed in were the floor exercise, parallel bars, rings, trampoline, and vault; their scores, in some order, were 10, 9, 8, 7, and 6.

T F

1. ☐ ☐ a) Primo competed on the parallel bars.
   ☐ ☐ b) Fabio competed on the rings.

2. ☐ ☐ a) The brother who scored a 10 competed in the floor exercise.
   ☐ ☐ b) Antonio scored an 8 in his event.

3. ☐ ☐ a) Primo's event was the trampoline.
   ☐ ☐ b) One brother scored a 7 in the floor exercise.

4. ☐ ☐ a) The brother who competed on the trampoline was Giacomo.
   ☐ ☐ b) There was a 10 scored on the parallel bars.

5. ☐ ☐ a) Marcello's score was lower than Giacomo's score.
   ☐ ☐ b) Primo's score was lower than Antonio's score.

6. ☐ ☐ a) Antonio competed on the rings.
   ☐ ☐ b) The score in the floor exercise was a 9.

7. ☐ ☐ a) The score in the trampoline event was lower than 9.
   ☐ ☐ b) The score in the vault event was higher than 7.

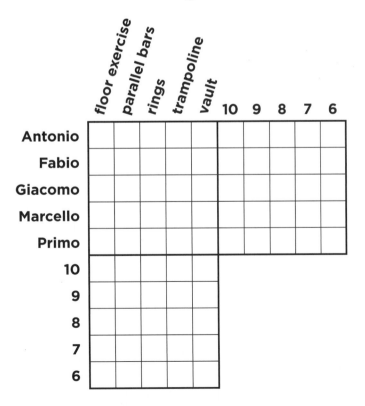

Investigators have determined that the Raviolis plan to rob the Twelfth National Bank sometime next week. We can ensure there's extra law enforcement there to intercept them, but it'll make our jobs (and the subsequent litigation) much easier if we can determine who's planning to do what. Of the six brothers, there is a driver, an inside man, a lookout, a safecracker, the "muscle," and the mastermind behind the whole operation.

Coinflip gave us the following statements about the bank heist; they're bundled into his usual true/false pairs, and they're all inconveniently related to the Raviolis' gymnastics performances. However, having worked that information out already, you should be able to figure out which brother has which task for the big job.

(Note: A brother's "total score" is the sum of his scores at all of the meets he participated in.)

T F

1. ☐ ☐ a) The muscle scored lower than 7 at exactly one meet.
   ☐ ☐ b) The inside man's total score was 2 points higher than the driver's total score.

2. ☐ ☐ a) The mastermind received the same score at two different meets.
   ☐ ☐ b) The safecracker competed twice in one event and twice in another event.

3. ☐ ☐ a) The lookout received the same score at three different meets.
   ☐ ☐ b) The mastermind and the safecracker achieved the same total score.

4. ☐ ☐ a) The lookout and the driver each competed in four different events.
   ☐ ☐ b) The muscle and the inside man each competed in the same event at three different meets.

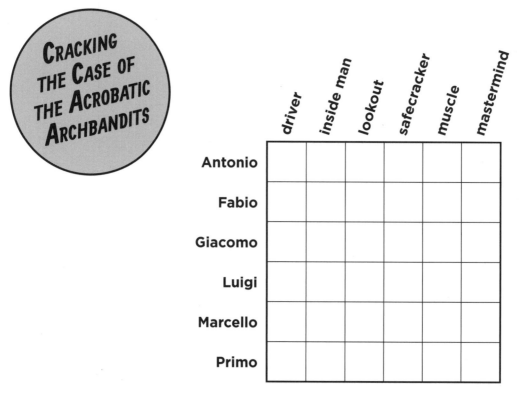

	driver	inside man	lookout	safecracker	muscle	mastermind
Antonio						
Fabio						
Giacomo						
Luigi						
Marcello						
Primo						

CRACKING THE CASE OF THE ACROBATIC ARCHBANDITS

THE CASE OF THE SECURITY IMPURITY

One of the nice things about solving crimes effectively in Enigmaville is that you command respect. Most local businesses don't bother wasting their profits on fancy top-of-the-line security systems, because they know if there's any wrongdoing, I'll see that justice is done in the end. After all, not only is electronic security expensive, but sometimes it's a lot more trouble than it's worth. Such was the case with last week's incident at Gulliver's Camera Supplies.

Ted Gulliver called up with a problem; he'd bought a security system from a new concern called Safe & Sound Security. It was a pretty extreme setup, as not only did the system monitor the store, but it also kept track of Ted's accounts, and it had the ability to lock them up if it detected a problem. On Monday morning, he discovered he had no access to his store's funds, and so he asked Safe & Sound to send over some technical support. When four guys from the company showed up, he was dismayed to recognize them as four customers who had been in the store every day the previous week acting suspicious. Getting the sense there might be something fishy going on, he immediately kicked them out and got me on the phone. Always a good move.

I'm not going to lie … computers are not my thing at all. As a result, the information I managed to extract from the system was sketchy at best, but here's how it looks to me. The security system was programmed to lock or unlock the accounts if fed a series of five passwords. The security geeks' plan was to visit the store and enter the passwords; I'm not totally sure what the next phase of the plan was, but it's likely that when unlocking the accounts, they would have tricked Ted into giving them some other secure data. The system keeps a record of which passwords were used, so they couldn't enter only the right ones. Thus, to throw any potential snoops off the trail, they each came in every day and entered two different passwords. Well, this particular snoop managed to scrape some additional info off the server. Figuring out who entered which passwords would be a good first step to figuring out how to rescue Ted's accounts.

Instructions: For each puzzle, determine which two passwords were entered by each of the four employees (Dexter, Eugene, Lloyd, and Norbert) on the given day; each password was used by exactly one employee. Two passwords are said to "share" a letter if both passwords contain that letter, in any position. Two passwords are said to have a "matching" letter if they both contain the same letter in the same position. For example, the passwords CRAMP and PRICE share three letters (C, P, and R), but they have only one matching letter (the R).

Solutions for this chapter are on pages 86–88.

MONDAY

The passwords used on Monday were BEST, BORN, CLUB, FAWN, MIND, PIES, STEP, and WAND.

1. The first letter of one of Norbert's passwords appeared in at least one of Dexter's passwords.

2. Eugene's passwords shared exactly three letters with each other; so did Norbert's.

3. Lloyd's passwords shared no letters with each other.

4. The fourth letter of one of Dexter's passwords appeared in Dexter's other password.

	Password 1	Password 2
Dexter		
Eugene		
Lloyd		
Norbert		

PASSWORDS:

BEST

BORN

CLUB

FAWN

MIND

PIES

STEP

WAND

TUESDAY

The passwords used on Tuesday were CARD, CHAR, CHIP, GEAR, PLUM, READ, ROMP, and RUNT.

1. Norbert's passwords ended with the same letter.

2. Each of Dexter's passwords had a second letter that did not appear in Dexter's other password.

3. Eugene's passwords started with the same letter; so did Lloyd's.

4. One of Eugene's passwords had at least one matching letter with at least one of Norbert's passwords; the other had no matching letters with either of Norbert's passwords.

	Password 1	Password 2
Dexter		
Eugene		
Lloyd		
Norbert		

PASSWORDS:

CARD

CHAR

CHIP

GEAR

PLUM

READ

ROMP

RUNT

WEDNESDAY

The passwords used on Wednesday were CHASE, CHEAT, CLOVE, CRUST, SHORT, SLICE, SMART, and SPARE.

1. Each of the employees except for Lloyd used two passwords that had exactly two matching letters.

2. Dexter's passwords did not start with the same letter, and neither of them contained the letter I.

3. Norbert's passwords did not end with the same letter.

4. Lloyd's passwords shared at least one letter.

	Password 1	Password 2
Dexter		
Eugene		
Lloyd		
Norbert		

PASSWORDS:

CHASE

CHEAT

CLOVE

CRUST

SHORT

SLICE

SMART

SPARE

THURSDAY

The passwords used on Thursday were CLUMP, DRAIN, FRESH, PIERS, PLANK, PLEAD, SCARF, and TRICK.

1. The first letter of one of Lloyd's passwords was the fourth letter of Lloyd's other password.

2. No employee's two passwords had a matching second letter.

3. Eugene was the only employee whose passwords had a matching third letter.

4. Neither of Dexter's passwords came between Lloyd's passwords in alphabetical order.

	Password 1	Password 2
Dexter		
Eugene		
Lloyd		
Norbert		

PASSWORDS:

CLUMP

DRAIN

FRESH

PIERS

PLANK

PLEAD

SCARF

TRICK

FRIDAY

The passwords used on Friday were CAPTOR, COURTS, FRUITS, MASTER, PRIEST, SECTOR, STRIPE, and TRUISM.

1. Lloyd's passwords had the same fifth letter.

2. Norbert's passwords shared exactly two letters.

3. One of Eugene's passwords had a first letter earlier in the alphabet than the first letter of his other password, and also a last letter earlier in the alphabet than the last letter of his other password.

	Password 1	Password 2
Dexter		
Eugene		
Lloyd		
Norbert		

PASSWORDS:

CAPTOR

COURTS

FRUITS

MASTER

PRIEST

SECTOR

STRIPE

TRUISM

Having figured out who punched in which codes on all five days, we should now be on the verge of undoing this particular cybercrime. A fifth employee, Heinrich, was willing to sell out his crooked colleagues, and while his testimony should be enough to put them away, he claims not to know the account passwords. He did give us the information below, based on company policy, and hopefully with these guidelines, we can figure out the five codes that will reunite Ted Gulliver and his hard-earned cash.

1. Each of the five correct passwords was entered on a different day. Every employee entered one correct password, except for the ringleader, who entered two. The ringleader did not enter correct passwords on consecutive days.

2. No two correct passwords shared more than three letters.

3. No three correct passwords started with the same letter.

4. One correct password had a last letter that was the same as the first letter of the correct password entered the next day; neither of these passwords was entered by Norbert.

5. On two occasions, the correct password had the same last letter as the other password entered by the same employee that day.

6. Eugene did not enter a correct password on Wednesday.

CRACKING THE CASE OF THE SECURITY IMPURITY

	Correct password	Employee
Monday		
Tuesday		
Wednesday		
Thursday		
Friday		

THE CASE OF THE LOCOMOTIVE LOCO MOTIVE

There are a lot of reasons perps rob jewelry stores. Most of them want to fence diamonds for cash, and occasionally you'll run into a show-off who just wants to prove he can succeed where every other lowlife failed. But I don't think I've ever seen anyone driven in the same way as Charles "Railway" McTaggart. Railway's something of a romantic; he loves trains, and he's enamored with the old days when a gentleman crook would stealthily steal the goods, have a seat on the six o'clock express, and chug-a-chug off into the sunset. He's probably the only criminal I know who commits crimes for the thrill of the escape. Not that this comforts the proprietors of Gem of a Thing Jewelers, who showed up yesterday morning to find smashed cases and bits of a model train set, a sure sign that Railway's been by.

On the bright side, Railway's eccentric behavior gives us a lot of help when it comes to knowing where to find him. After all, Enigmaville only has train tracks leading to one place: South Cerebra. It would be a piece of cake to catch Railway if there were just one train he could be on, but in fact, trains head to South Cerebra nine times a day, every hour on the half-hour, from 8:30 in the morning to 4:30 in the afternoon. To make things even trickier, Railway does his homework. His MO is to find a group of similar passengers and disguise himself to blend in.

Asking around, we rounded up five groups of related suspects who were catching trains on the day of the crime. Each of them had a story for why they were taking the train, but one of them is sure to be an impostor. It'd be more helpful if they were giving us more information (none of them were thrilled about having their travel plans interrupted), but I think we may have extracted enough to figure out exactly when they traveled, which should in turn help us work out which one robbed the jewelry store.

Instructions: For each puzzle, determine which of the suspects was on which train, and another piece of information about each suspect's trip. Trains depart at 8:30 A.M., 9:30 A.M., 10:30 A.M., 11:30 A.M., 12:30 P.M., 1:30 P.M., 2:30 P.M., 3:30 P.M., and 4:30 P.M. No two suspects in the same puzzle were on the same train.

Solutions for this chapter are on pages 88–90.

SUSPECT GROUP 1

Five suspects claimed to be on their way home from a vacation. The suspects' names were Karl, Leonard, Mitch, Nate, and Orville. Each of them was returning from a different island paradise: Aruba, Jamaica, Bermuda, the Bahamas, or Key Largo.

1. Leonard's train was four hours later than the Jamaica vacationer's train, which did not leave at 12:30 P.M.

2. Mitch and the vacationer from the Bahamas both left in the morning. The other three vacationers (Orville, Karl, and the one coming from Bermuda) left in the afternoon.

3. One vacationer left an hour after Nate, and was the last vacationer to leave before Karl did.

4. One vacationer (who did not have the latest departure of the five) left three hours after the vacationer coming from Key Largo.

	name	island paradise
8:30 A.M.		
9:30 A.M.		
10:30 A.M.		
11:30 A.M.		
12:30 P.M.		
1:30 P.M.		
2:30 P.M.		
3:30 P.M.		
4:30 P.M.		

SUSPECT GROUP 2

Five suspects were allegedly lawyers from the Law Offices of Sons & Sons, surnamed Anderson, Goodson, Harrison, Johnson, and Simpson. Each of them carried their legal briefs inside a different carry-on: an attaché case, a duffel bag, a fanny pack, a knapsack, and a rollaboard.

1. The lawyer with the duffel bag left three hours after Anderson and one hour before Goodson.

2. One lawyer (not Anderson) left one hour before the train carrying a lawyer with an attaché case.

3. Simpson left one hour after the lawyer with the knapsack and two hours before Johnson.

4. Harrison left five hours before the lawyer who had the fanny pack.

	name	carry-on
8:30 A.M.		
9:30 A.M.		
10:30 A.M.		
11:30 A.M.		
12:30 P.M.		
1:30 P.M.		
2:30 P.M.		
3:30 P.M.		
4:30 P.M.		

SUSPECT GROUP 3

Six suspects were apparently on their way to a costume convention where they intended to portray pirates, using the names Captain Dread, Captain Fear, Captain Fright, Captain Nightmare, Captain Shock, and Captain Terror. However, having blown all their money on the convention fee, each could only afford one element of a costume: an eyepatch, a hat, a parrot, a pegleg, a plank, and a sword.

1. No three consecutive trains before 2 P.M. all had pirates on them.

2. The pirate with the hat left one hour after Captain Shock (who was not on the 3:30 P.M. train).

3. The pirate with the plank left six hours before Captain Nightmare, who did not have an eyepatch.

4. Three hours after Captain Fright's train left, another train left without a pirate on it.

5. Captain Dread's train was two hours earlier than the train carrying the pirate with a sword.

6. Captain Fear left on the 2:30 P.M. train, while the pirate with the pegleg left at 9:30 A.M.

	name	costume element
8:30 A.M.		
9:30 A.M.		
10:30 A.M.		
11:30 A.M.		
12:30 P.M.		
1:30 P.M.		
2:30 P.M.		
3:30 P.M.		
4:30 P.M.		

SUSPECT GROUP 4

Six of the suspects were dressed as clowns and said that since there was too much competition on the birthday party circuit, they were each on their way to try working a new event. The clowns' names were Giggles, Hilarity, Kabonk, Slappy, Toodles, and Yukster, and they were hired for a bachelor party, a baptism, a bar mitzvah, a graduation, a retirement party, and a wedding.

1. Slappy left before the baptism clown, who left before the wedding clown, who left before Giggles.

2. The wedding clown left four hours later than the graduation clown.

3. The retirement party clown and graduation clown were on consecutive trains (in some order); two other clowns, Yukster and Toodles, were on another pair of trains that were also consecutive (in some order).

4. The bachelor party clown left after Kabonk, who left after Hilarity, who left after the bar mitzvah clown.

5. Toodles left four hours earlier than Giggles.

	name	event
8:30 A.M.		
9:30 A.M.		
10:30 A.M.		
11:30 A.M.		
12:30 P.M.		
1:30 P.M.		
2:30 P.M.		
3:30 P.M.		
4:30 P.M.		

SUSPECT GROUP 5

Seven suspects claimed to be fashion designers named Ilsa, Kyra, Minerva, Natasha, Paula, Vera, and Zelda. All of them were on their way to a fashion show, transporting their newest creations: a little red dress, a little orange dress, a little yellow dress, a little green dress, a little blue dress, a little indigo dress, and a little violet dress.

1. The designer with the little violet dress left before the designer with the little orange dress.

2. Paula left an hour after the designer with the little yellow dress, who left sometime in the afternoon.

3. Kyra and Zelda were on consecutive trains (in some order).

4. One designer left one hour before and one hour after trains with no designers on them.

5. Ilsa's train was three hours after the train with the little red dress.

6. Two hours after a train left with a little green dress, another train left with no designer.

7. At least one designer left between the departures of the designers with the little red dress and little blue dress (in some order).

8. Minerva was on the 12:30 P.M. train.

9. Natasha and Kyra had the little orange dress and little blue dress (in some order).

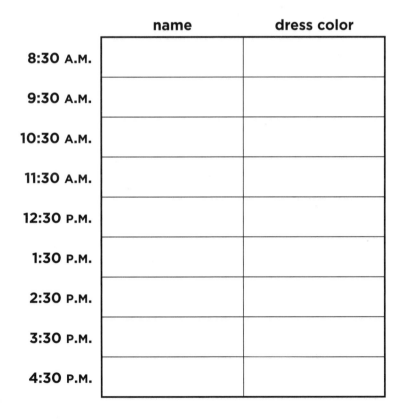

	name	dress color
8:30 A.M.		
9:30 A.M.		
10:30 A.M.		
11:30 A.M.		
12:30 P.M.		
1:30 P.M.		
2:30 P.M.		
3:30 P.M.		
4:30 P.M.		

Twenty-nine suspects is a whole lot of suspects, but we were able to amass a collection of rather strange leads to narrow down the possibilities. Combined with our information on who rode what train, it should be enough information to figure out which suspect was Railway in disguise.

1. Railway was not on the train carrying exactly two suspects.

2. Railway was not on the train carrying a clown but not a pirate.

3. Railway was not on the train carrying a vacationer and designer whose first names had the same number of letters.

4. Railway was not on the train carrying neither a clown nor a designer.

5. Railway was not on the train carrying a dress of a color with the same number of letters as a pirate accessory on board.

6. Railway was not on the train carrying a lawyer and a vacationer but not a pirate.

7. Railway was not on the train that was not carrying a lawyer and that left immediately after a train not carrying a pirate.

8. Railway was not on the train carrying a clown and a vacationer whose names had exactly one letter in common.

9. Railway's cover name did not contain the first letter of the name of the vacationer on the train carrying the lawyer with the attaché case.

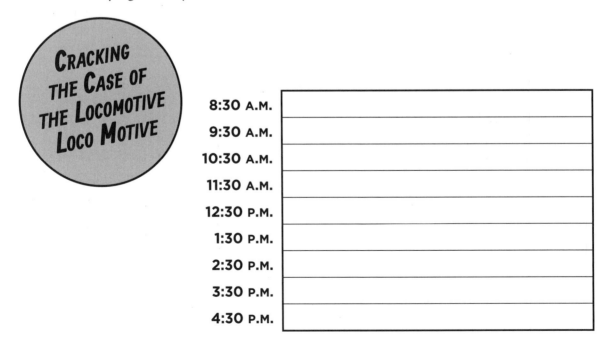

CRACKING THE CASE OF THE LOCOMOTIVE Loco Motive

8:30 A.M.	
9:30 A.M.	
10:30 A.M.	
11:30 A.M.	
12:30 P.M.	
1:30 P.M.	
2:30 P.M.	
3:30 P.M.	
4:30 P.M.	

THE CASE OF THE CROOKED CRASHERS

You know, it's been thirty years now, and I still want my bicycle back. When I was just a kid, I had waited all year for a shiny new BMX bike, so that I could ride around the neighborhood and nab perps. It was the centerpiece of my birthday party that year; I hadn't opened the present yet, but it's pretty hard to hide a bicycle with wrapping paper and scotch tape. In fact, I never did get to open it, because somebody rode off with it while I was blowing out my candles. All my friends were in the room at the time, so whoever rode my bike away had showed up uninvited.

But I digress. The point is that, all these years later, if there's one thing I can't stand, it's a party crasher. And if there's another thing I can't stand, it's anybody who steals vehicles. So you can imagine how much my blood boiled when I heard the suspects in an auto theft crime wave were known for showing up at parties uninvited.

Five cars were stolen in one of the more upscale suburbs of Enigmaville last weekend, which is a pretty high disappearance rate for that part of town. Nobody could put the pieces together until I noticed there was a Halloween party near every theft. We questioned the attendees and figured out that five people—Adam, Bret, Cora, Drew, and Erin—showed up every night, conspicuously wearing many of the same costumes. I figure at least one of them must have been making off with people's rides.

We questioned all five of the suspects about the parties, and an interesting thing happened: when a suspect was talking about a party, every one of their statements was true if they were invited, and every statement was false if they were crashing. A weird phenomenon, but at least they're consistent, and it makes it possible to figure out pretty much everything you need to know.

Instructions: For each puzzle, determine which of the suspects wore which costume to which party; for the third, fourth, and fifth parties, also determine what beverage they brought with them. For each party, if a suspect was invited to a party, each of their statements is true; if they were crashing (not invited), their statements are false.

Solutions for this chapter are on pages 90–91.

THE FIRST PARTY

At the first party, the suspects dressed as a cat, a devil, a ghost, a gorilla, and a vampire.

T F

1. Adam said: ☐ ☐ a) Cora dressed as a gorilla.
   ☐ ☐ b) Erin dressed as either a cat or a devil.

2. Bret said: ☐ ☐ a) The devil was either Cora or Erin.
   ☐ ☐ b) At most two of the five of us were invited to the party.

3. Cora said: ☐ ☐ a) Bret was the one dressed as a vampire.
   ☐ ☐ b) Adam and Erin were both uninvited.

4. Drew said: ☐ ☐ a) Bret's costume was either a ghost or a cat.
   ☐ ☐ b) Adam came to the party as a vampire.

5. Erin said: ☐ ☐ a) The person dressed as a ghost was either Adam or me.
   ☐ ☐ b) Bret and Drew were both invited.

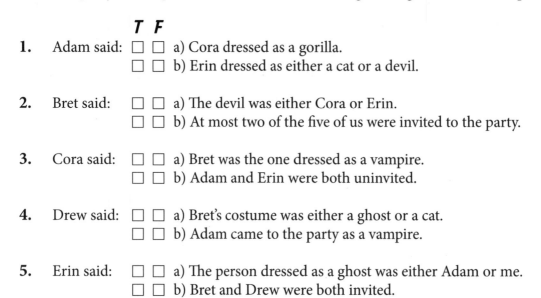

THE SECOND PARTY

At the second party, the suspects dressed as a cat, a devil, a gorilla, a police officer, and a zombie.

T F

1. Adam said: ☐ ☐ a) Drew was dressed as either a cat or a devil.
   ☐ ☐ b) Cora was dressed as either a gorilla or a zombie.

2. Bret said: ☐ ☐ a) The person dressed as a police officer was crashing.
   ☐ ☐ b) Adam was either the gorilla or the police officer.

3. Cora said: ☐ ☐ a) Bret was either the devil or the zombie.
   ☐ ☐ b) My costume was either a cat or a police officer.

4. Drew said: ☐ ☐ a) Bret showed up dressed as a cat.
   ☐ ☐ b) I was either the gorilla or the police officer.

5. Erin said: ☐ ☐ a) Bret was either the gorilla or the police officer.
   ☐ ☐ b) Cora wasn't dressed as a zombie.
   ☐ ☐ c) The cat wasn't Adam.

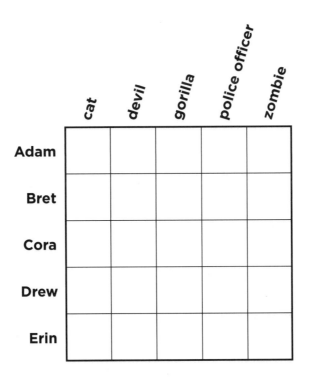

THE THIRD PARTY

At the third party, the suspects dressed as a ghost, a gorilla, a police officer, a vampire, and a zombie. They also each brought a different beverage: beer, rum, soda, tequila, or wine.

T F

1. Adam said:
    - ☐ ☐ a) The person dressed as a police officer brought rum.
    - ☐ ☐ b) I didn't bring beer or tequila.
    - ☐ ☐ c) Nobody invited Bret to the party.

2. Bret said:
    - ☐ ☐ a) I brought neither soda nor wine.
    - ☐ ☐ b) Erin showed up dressed as a ghost.
    - ☐ ☐ c) The vampire brought soda.

3. Cora said:
    - ☐ ☐ a) The person who brought beer was in a gorilla costume.
    - ☐ ☐ b) Adam wasn't crashing the party.
    - ☐ ☐ c) I didn't bring rum or tequila.

4. Drew said:
    - ☐ ☐ a) The drink Erin brought was either tequila or beer.
    - ☐ ☐ b) I didn't bring soda or tequila.
    - ☐ ☐ c) The person in the ghost costume was invited.

5. Erin said:
    - ☐ ☐ a) Drew was an uninvited guest.
    - ☐ ☐ b) I didn't bring rum or wine with me.
    - ☐ ☐ c) Bret's costume was either a gorilla or a vampire.

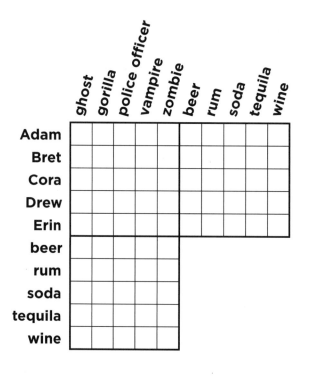

THE FOURTH PARTY

At the fourth party, the suspects dressed as a devil, a gorilla, a police officer, a vampire, and a zombie. They again each brought a different beverage: beer, rum, soda, tequila, or wine.

T F

1. Adam said:
    - ☐ ☐ a) The zombie brought either beer or wine.
    - ☐ ☐ b) Erin was dressed as either a vampire or a police officer.
    - ☐ ☐ c) Drew didn't bring soda.

2. Bret said:
    - ☐ ☐ a) I brought tequila with me.
    - ☐ ☐ b) Exactly two of the five of us were invited to the party.
    - ☐ ☐ c) Either the vampire or the zombie brought beer.

3. Cora said:
    - ☐ ☐ a) The police officer's drink was neither beer nor wine.
    - ☐ ☐ b) Erin's costume was a devil, a zombie, or a gorilla.
    - ☐ ☐ c) Exactly two of the five of us were crashing the party.

4. Drew said:
    - ☐ ☐ a) The person in the gorilla costume was either Bret or Cora.
    - ☐ ☐ b) Adam brought rum, soda, or wine.

5. Erin said:
    - ☐ ☐ a) Bret wore a devil costume.
    - ☐ ☐ b) Of the other four suspects, an odd number of them crashed the party.

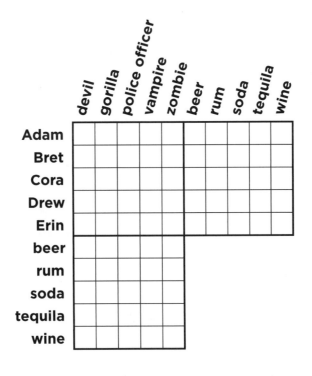

THE FIFTH PARTY

At the fifth party, the suspects dressed as a cat, a devil, a ghost, a vampire, and a zombie. And yet again, they each brought a different beverage: beer, rum, soda, tequila, or wine.

T F

1. Adam said:
   - ☐ ☐ a) I brought rum with me to the party.
   - ☐ ☐ b) The person who wore a cat costume was an invited guest.
   - ☐ ☐ c) Drew and Erin were not both invited to the party.

2. Bret said:
   - ☐ ☐ a) I brought wine with me to the party.
   - ☐ ☐ b) Erin did not dress as a zombie.
   - ☐ ☐ c) Exactly one of the five of us crashed the party.

3. Cora said:
   - ☐ ☐ a) I brought soda with me to the party.
   - ☐ ☐ b) Adam brought tequila.
   - ☐ ☐ c) The person in the devil costume was invited to the party.

4. Drew said:
   - ☐ ☐ a) I brought beer with me to the party.
   - ☐ ☐ b) Cora's costume was either a cat or a vampire.
   - ☐ ☐ c) Adam wasn't dressed as a ghost.

5. Erin said:
   - ☐ ☐ a) I brought tequila with me to the party.
   - ☐ ☐ b) The person who brought soda was dressed as a devil.
   - ☐ ☐ c) Of the five of us, the number of invited guests was not exactly two.

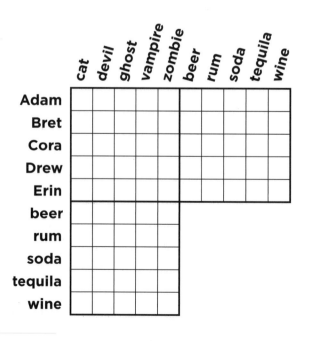

Having worked out the details of the suspects' behaviors at the parties, we dragged some additional information out of them to try to determine who was involved with the car thefts, and who just had lousy manners. Not surprisingly, anyone who was a car thief made a false statement, whereas anyone who was innocent told the truth. Let's see if we can use this testimony to work out who's responsible for the vanishing vehicles.

T F

1. Adam said: ☐ ☐ Exactly one thief brought the same beverage to two different parties.

2. Bret said: ☐ ☐ At the last three parties, anyone who was a thief either brought the same beverage twice or wore the same costume twice.

3. Cora said: ☐ ☐ The person who dressed as a police officer more than once and the person who dressed as a vampire more than once were either both thieves or both innocent.

4. Drew said: ☐ ☐ At least one thief wore the same costume to two consecutive parties.

5. Erin said: ☐ ☐ At least one thief wore the same costume to three different parties.

CRACKING THE CASE OF THE CROOKED CRASHERS

	thoroughly thievish	purely a party-hopper
Adam		
Bret		
Cora		
Drew		
Erin		

THE CASE OF THE SECONDHAND SECOND HANDS

Different neighborhoods of Enigmaville gain renown for different reasons, whether it's the friendly people, the delicious food, or (sad to say) the dastardly crimes committed there. For example, you'd think the Coordinate District would be known for its simply designed street layout, or for the excellent pork dumplings you can get on the corner of 3rd & F. Instead, in recent times, it's become notorious for a seedier reason: it's by far the best spot in the city to buy stolen watches, thanks to a gang of seven hot watch dealers who relocate from street corner to street corner every day.

We've spent months trying to nab the gang, but they're sneaky and hard to get a bead on. To make matters worse, if we try to bust one of them, the other six are likely to get away. As tempting as it is to arrest a dealer as soon as we locate one, the only way to truly fix this problem is to arrest everyone at once, which involves knowing where all seven dealers are going to be ahead of time.

Luckily, at the beginning of this week, we hit paydirt. An informant, clearly disappointed by his unimpressive kickbacks from Rolex resales, agreed to monitor the dealers' behavior throughout the week and give us some additional notes to predict where they'd be on Saturday. Admittedly, his descriptions are spotty and cryptic, but it should be enough to figure out where the seven dealers were each day from Monday through Friday, and then to figure out where they'll be on Saturday so we can run these terrible timekeeper tyrants right out of town.

Instructions: For each puzzle, determine which corner of the Coordinate District each of seven counterfeit watch dealers (Archie, Biff, Calvin, Dwight, Earl, Frank, and Garrett) worked on that day. The Coordinate District consists of seven north-south avenues, counting up from the westernmost 1st Avenue to the easternmost 7th Avenue, all of which cross seven west-east streets, which run from the northernmost A Street to the southernmost G Street. The word "street" always refers

to a street, not an avenue, and vice versa. The distance between two corners is the shortest total number of blocks one has to travel (moving horizontally and vertically) to get from one block to the other. The word "directly" implies a straight line of any distance in a given direction; for example, 5th & A is directly northeast of 2nd & D, but 5th & B is not.

Solutions for this chapter are on pages 91–94.

MONDAY

1. Earl (whose corner was directly northeast of Frank's) was further east than Biff (who was exactly ten blocks away from Calvin).

2. Frank and Garrett were the only two dealers that worked on the same street; one of them was three blocks east of the other.

3. From Archie's corner, you could get to Garrett's corner by traveling two blocks east and three blocks south.

4. Dwight, who worked on F Street, was the only dealer on his avenue. One of the other dealers, who owed him money, worked closer to Dwight than any other dealer did.

5. Calvin worked on 2nd Avenue, where he was less than three blocks away from another dealer.

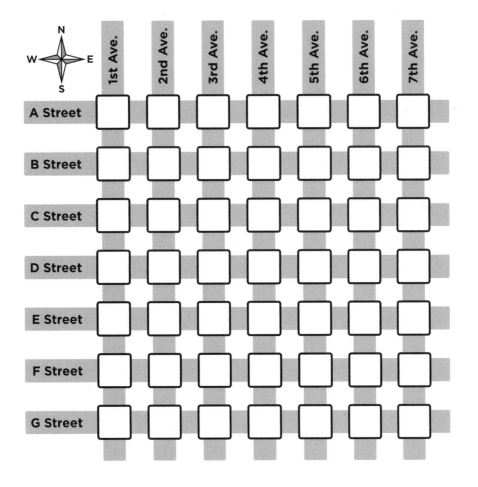

TUESDAY

1. As a professional courtesy, each dealer worked on a different street, and each worked on a different avenue.

2. Earl and Garrett worked on 2nd and 3rd Avenue, in some order. Meanwhile, Calvin and Frank worked on A Street and F Street, in some order; neither of them was stationed on 4th Avenue.

3. Dwight was directly northwest of Archie (who was at least six blocks away from Frank). Dwight was also directly northeast of at least one dealer.

4. At some point a cop poked around at 4th and E (where there was no dealer), which made Calvin and Garrett nervous since they were both the same distance from that corner. Biff, who was exactly three times as far away from the cop, was less concerned.

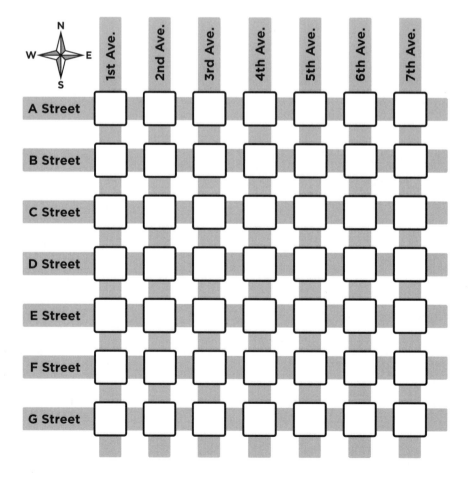

WEDNESDAY

1. In reaction to the police presence the day before, the dealers set up an emergency communication chain. In case of danger, Earl warned a second dealer who was standing on the same street or avenue. The second dealer then warned a third who was standing on the same street or avenue as the second, and so on until the seventh dealer, Calvin, was informed. This chain alternated between streets and avenues. No three dealers were on one street or avenue.

2. Frank (who was on either 3rd Avenue or 7th Avenue) was directly northeast of Biff (who was on either D Street or F Street).

3. There were exactly three dealers north of D Street; all three of these dealers were positioned west of 5th Avenue, and they were not the first three dealers in the communication chain.

4. Garrett was exactly twice as far away from Biff as Earl was.

5. Dwight's corner was directly west of Calvin's corner, exactly five blocks away. Calvin was directly southeast of some dealer who wasn't Archie.

6. Archie and Garrett were on corners exactly three blocks apart, and there was exactly one dealer between them in the communication chain.

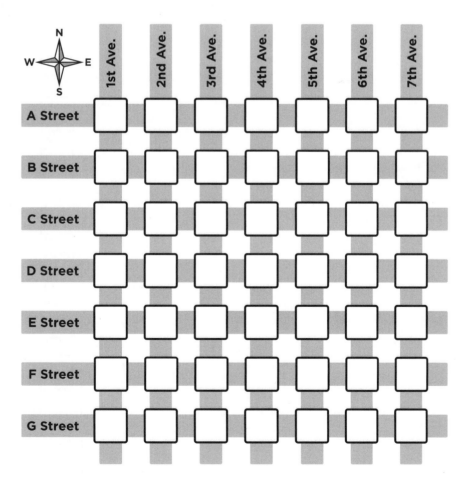

THURSDAY

1. On Thursday, the dealers each employed a different assistant (Jacques, Kevin, Luke, Moe, Nero, Oliver, and Patrick). Each dealer's assistant stood at the same corner as the dealer.

2. Repeating Tuesday's experiment, each dealer worked on a different street, and each worked on a different avenue.

3. Earl stood exactly eleven blocks away from Dwight, and more than five blocks away from Nero.

4. Jacques and Patrick worked on F Street and 7th Avenue in some order, while Biff and Garrett worked on C Street and 4th Avenue in some order.

5. If you started at Frank's corner and walked three blocks east and one block north, you'd arrive at Kevin's corner.

6. One dealer worked at 2nd & D; it wasn't Calvin, whose assistant was Oliver.

7. Luke and Moe, neither of whom worked on B Street, worked exactly four blocks apart. Luke's corner was further north than Garrett's.

8. Archie worked on G Street. He was not exactly three blocks away from Jacques's corner.

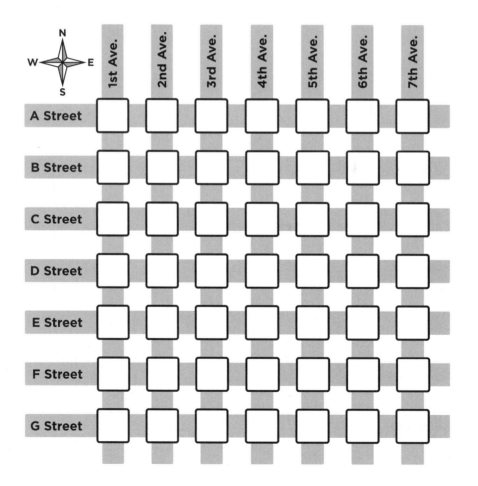

FRIDAY

1. The seven dealers employed the same seven assistants as on Thursday, though each assistant may or may not have assisted the same dealer as before.

2. Calvin's corner was three blocks north and four blocks west of Moe's corner, while Oliver's corner was one block west and four blocks south of Biff's corner.

3. Archie and Nero worked together on 5th Avenue. Frank and Kevin worked together on D Street, at a corner the same distance from Patrick's corner as it was from another dealer (who worked directly south of yet another dealer).

4. Exactly three dealers all worked on the same street; the other four all worked on different streets from each other.

5. Jacques's corner was two blocks west and two blocks north of Garrett's corner, and it was also two blocks east and two blocks south of Earl's corner.

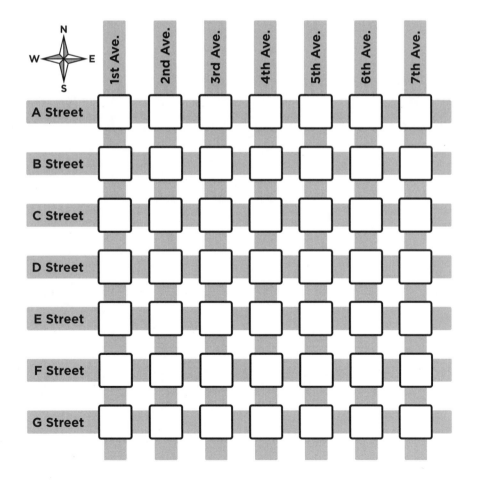

Now that we know the positions of the seven dealers throughout the week, we can combine that information with our informant's insights, figure out where the dealers are going to be tomorrow, and bust them once and for all.

1. No dealer will be on any street or avenue that he was on one of the five previous days.

2. The dealer whose corners on Monday and Tuesday were the greatest distance apart will be directly northwest of one of those two corners.

3. The dealers who worked with Moe on Thursday and Friday will be on the same street as each other, but they will not be on adjacent corners.

4. No three dealers will be on the same street, or on the same avenue.

5. The second dealer in Wednesday's chain of communication will be exactly five blocks from his Monday location. Every other dealer will be at least two blocks away from him.

6. One of the assistants worked on the same avenue on Thursday and Friday; one dealer will be on the corner of that avenue and F Street.

7. Two dealers were on the same avenue on Monday. Of these two dealers, one of them will be directly south of the dealer who was southernmost on Tuesday. The other will be directly north of the dealer who was easternmost on Wednesday.

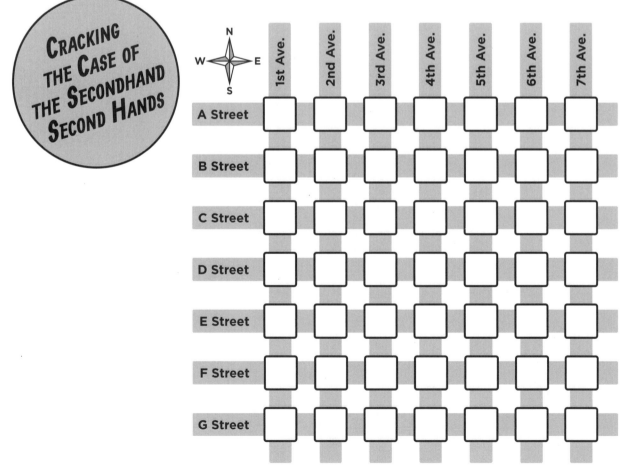

THE CASE OF THE VAULT ASSAULT

Every now and then, we get a call from one of Enigmaville's finer banks, telling us they've been robbed. And then when we ask what was taken, they say they don't know. That's when I know Mac Hacker is back in town.

Mac Hacker's one of the most skilled safecrackers ever to land on the wrong side of the law. But most of the time, emptying a vault isn't enough for him; he insists on resealing it with a lock of his own devising. That way, not only does he get away with the goods, he gets to go to sleep laughing his head off, knowing that when the authorities show up, they're not going to be able to open what he opened with ease.

Mac's outdone himself this time though. Five banks in one night, that's hardly a record. On the other hand, it's not every day you walk into your own office and find what looks like an active bomb stuffed inside a transparent (yet disturbingly secure) safe. The combination lock prompts for a seven-digit sequence with no repeats, so at least there are only 604,800 possible combos to worry about. (What? A good combinatorics class is part of any decent detective training program.) I could start trying them all, but I don't know if we have that kind of time, and more importantly, I don't want to know what happens if you input an incorrect code.

On the bright side, Mac has a bit of a Riddler complex, and I've already heard that he left some clues outside each of the bank vaults. I don't see any here, but I wouldn't be surprised if each of those vaults contains more clues about the combination to the last safe. And I certainly hope my hunch is right, because honestly, I haven't really come up with a backup plan.

Instructions: For each puzzle, determine the seven-digit vault combination. Each of the seven positions can hold any digit from 0 to 9, but no digit appears more than once in a single combination.

Solutions for this chapter are on pages 94–96.

THE ERIE STREET BANK

1. The sum of the first and fifth digits is the same as the sum of the third and fourth digits.

2. The second digit is twice as large as the fifth digit, while the fourth digit is twice as large as the second digit.

3. The sum of the first two digits is the same as the product of two other digits of the combination.

4. The first digit is twice as large as the sixth digit.

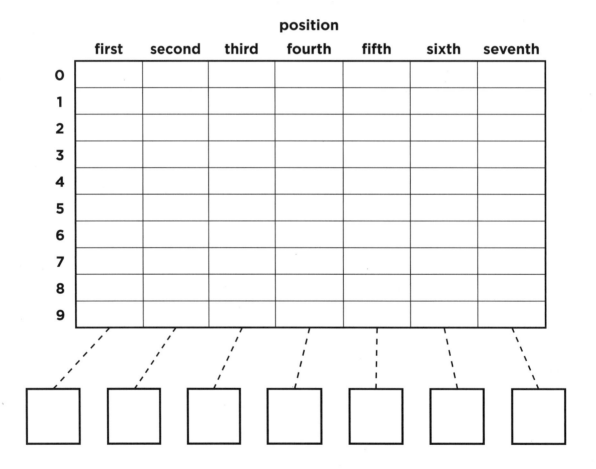

THE HURON STREET BANK

1. Every adjacent pair of digits differs by either two or three.

2. No set of four adjacent digits consists of four consecutive numbers (in any order).

3. The two-digit number formed by the last two digits is an exact multiple of the two-digit number formed by the first two digits; neither of these numbers begins with a zero.

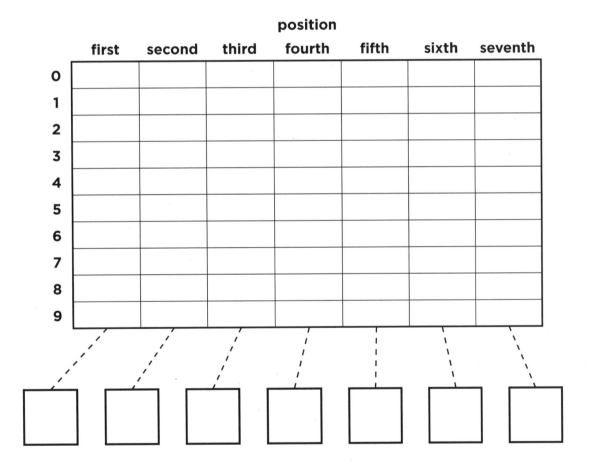

THE MICHIGAN STREET BANK

1. The first three digits are increasing from left to right, but when written in English, they are in alphabetical order from right to left. (For reference, the alphabetized list of digits is: eight, five, four, nine, one, seven, six, three, two, zero.)

2. The middle three digits (the third, fourth, and fifth) are increasing from right to left, but when written in English, they are in alphabetical order from left to right.

3. The last three digits are increasing from left to right, but when written in English, they are in alphabetical order from right to left.

4. The seventh digit is the sum of the first, second, and fourth digits.

5. Of the six pairs of adjacent digits, only one of them is a pair of consecutive digits (in either order).

6. The sixth digit is two more than the third digit.

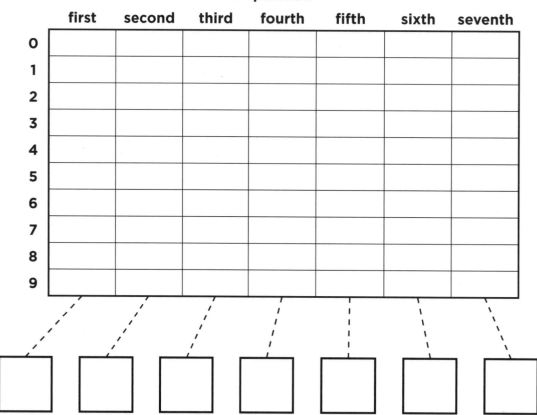

72

THE ONTARIO STREET BANK

1. When written in English, the first and second digits do not share any letters in common.

2. When written in English, the third and fourth digits do not share any letters in common.

3. When written in English, the fifth and sixth digits do not share any letters in common.

4. The smallest even digit in the combination is adjacent to the largest odd digit.

5. The second digit is one more than the seventh digit, and the fourth digit is one more than the fifth digit.

6. There is exactly one pair of digits in the combination with a sum of 12; at least one of these two digits is either the first or last digit in the combination.

7. The second and fifth digits in the combination are both odd.

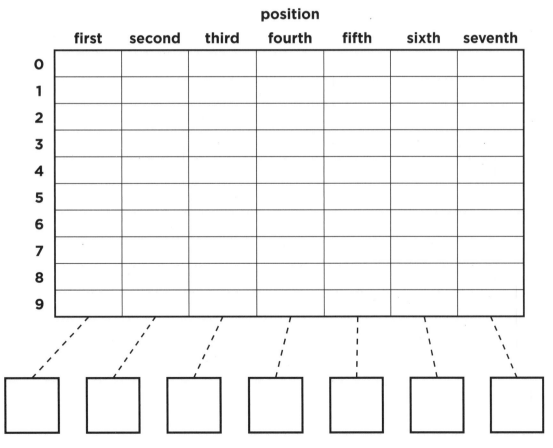

THE SUPERIOR STREET BANK

1. Of the second and fifth digits, one is three times as large as the other.

2. The third and sixth digits differ by five.

3. Of the fourth and seventh digits, one is four times as large as the other.

4. The first digit is larger than the sixth digit.

5. It would be possible to change four of the digits in the combination (without changing their order) so that the result is a sequence of seven consecutive digits in increasing order.

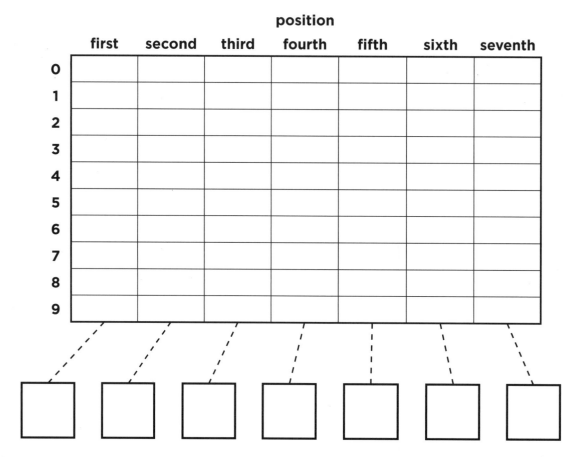

Well, that's the last time I put the intern in charge of evidence collection. There was indeed a slip of paper inside each of the five vaults, and surprisingly there was nothing missing from any of the vaults. I don't want to be egotistical, but it seems like this was all about me. All of the clues refer to a "master combination," which presumably can open the safe in my office just before it explodes.

But now, thanks to the intern, we have no record of which slip was in which vault ... which is a big problem, given that each of them refers to the combination from its own vault. It might still be possible to work out the master combination, but first we'll need to figure out which slip is which.

Note: A digit in one combination "matches" a digit in another combination if the two combinations have the same digit in the same position.

Slip 1:

a) The second digit of the master combination is one less than the second digit of this vault's combination.

b) The number of digits in this vault's combination that match digits in the master combination is odd.

CRACKING THE CASE OF THE VAULT ASSAULT

Slip 2:

a) The sum of the digits in the master combination is six more than the sum of the digits in this vault's combination.

b) None of the digits in this vault's combination match digits in the master combination.

Slip 3:

a) The sixth digit of the master combination differs from the sixth digit of this vault's combination by one.

b) The second digit of this vault's combination is one less than the second digit of the master combination.

Slip 4:

a) Of the sixth digit of the master combination and the sixth digit of this vault's combination, one is even and one is odd.

b) The fourth digit of the master combination differs from the fourth digit of this vault's combination by three.

Slip 5:

a) The third digit of the master combination differs from the third digit of this vault's combination by one.

b) The number of digits in this vault's combination that match digits in the master combination is odd.

Master combination:

☐ ☐ ☐ ☐ ☐ ☐ ☐

A DISTURBING LETTER

Dear Thorn in My Side,

After orchestrating a massive crime wave certain to outwit the puny brain of Lieutenant Larry Logic, I was dismayed to watch him foil my plans again and again, thanks to your infuriating assistance. Without you, he would have finally failed and lost the faith of the city. Thanks to your help, he is instead more popular than ever.

Well, I have decided to take the kid gloves off and take the good lieutenant away. I am not fond of violence, so I assure you he is quite safe. But if you are unable to unravel the clues in this letter and determine my true identity, I'm afraid it will be a very long time before he solves another crime for the helpless populace of Enigmaville.

In recent weeks, you have managed to arrest five of my right-hand men: Mario Desmond, Mac Hacker, Charles McTaggart, Giacomo Ravioli, and Norbert Spader. Each of these men has a codename (Alpha, Bravo, Charlie, Delta, or Echo) and two passcodes, a primary and a secondary (each a positive whole number). In the clues that follow, you will notice a series of letters where you would expect to see numbers. The numbers these letters represent are as follows:

- A is the sum of the digits represented by ham and bacon at Mario's Calzones, minus the digit represented by meatballs.
- B is the total number of *Galactic Conflict VII* showings attended by the only smuggler that attended more 6 P.M. showings than midnight showings.
- C is the number of your suspects who were on Railway McTaggart's train (including Railway).
- D is the number of same-gender pairs of substitute teachers who met up after being questioned about the Phantom.
- E is the score that the Ravioli Brothers' safecracker earned at a meet immediately after a meet at which the mastermind earned the same score.
- F is the sum of every digit in Mac Hacker's master combination that is lower than the digit immediately to its right.
- G is the number of Halloween parties to which at least one car thief was invited.
- H is the distance (in Coordinate District blocks) between Biff's Saturday location and Garrett's Saturday location.
- I is the number of letters of the alphabet that appear in at least two of the correct passwords for Ted Gulliver's accounts.
- J is the number of LeBleu auctions at which David Chartreuse spent more than William Puce and Richard Umber combined.

If you dare to try, use these clues to determine the codenames and passcodes of each of the five men. If you manage to work them out, put the names in order by codename. For each man in turn, read the letter of the man's full name that corresponds to his primary passcode. (For example, if Norbert Spader were Alpha, and his primary passcode were 9, you would read the 9th letter of his full name, which is P.) Then do the same with the secondary passcodes. The resulting phrase will reveal my identity; any subsequent department paperwork is your own problem.

Deviously,
The Boss

1. No two men have the same primary passcode, no two men have the same secondary passcode, and no man's primary passcode is the same as his secondary passcode.

2. The difference between the highest and lowest secondary passcodes is A.

3. The sum of Bravo's two passcodes is a multiple of B.

4. The sum of Mario Desmond's two passcodes is a multiple of C.

5. The only primary passcodes such that one is exactly D times the other belong to Charles McTaggart and Echo. Both of these passcodes are higher than Alpha's primary passcode.

6. The largest number that is either a primary or secondary passcode but not the other is E.

7. The smallest number that is either a primary or secondary passcode but not the other is F.

8. Delta's secondary passcode is one more than G times Giacomo Ravioli's secondary passcode.

9. Mac Hacker's secondary passcode is a multiple of H.

10. The sum of the two smallest primary passcodes is I.

11. Echo's secondary passcode is J more than Mario Desmond's secondary passcode.

codename	real name	primary passcode	secondary passcode
ALPHA			
BRAVO			
CHARLIE			
DELTA			
ECHO			

Solution is on page 96.

SOLUTIONS

THE CASE OF THE SUBSTANDARD SUBSTITUTE

SUSPECT GROUP 1

Byron taught at Garfield (#3), and since Bert didn't teach at Kennedy (#2), he taught at Polk and Bob taught at Kennedy. Bert, who taught at Polk, taught history (#3), and since Bob, who taught at Kennedy, didn't teach math (#2), he taught science and Byron taught math. Bob's last name is Bundy (#4), and since Byron, the math teacher, isn't Mr. Bradley (#4), he is Mr. Bell and Bert is Mr. Bradley.

Bert Bradley taught history at Polk.
Bob Bundy taught science at Kennedy.
Byron Bell taught math at Garfield.

SUSPECT GROUP 2

The Spanish class was at Kennedy (#2), and since the class at Coolidge was neither history (#3) nor literature (#5), it was science. Since Daria didn't teach at Coolidge (#5), she didn't teach science. She also didn't teach history (#3) or literature (#5), so she taught Spanish. Ms. Dryden isn't Daria (#5), so she didn't teach at Kennedy; neither did Ms. Dickson (#3) nor Ms. Dunn (#2), so Ms. Dedham taught at Kennedy. The Coolidge teacher wasn't Ms. Dedham, Ms. Dickson (#3), or Ms. Dryden (#5), so she was Ms. Dunn, whose first name is Diana (#2). That means Delia didn't teach at Coolidge, so she taught at Roosevelt (#4) and Dolores taught at Polk. Since Dolores didn't teach history (#3), she taught literature and Delia taught history; and since Ms. Dickson didn't teach history (#3), Delia is Ms. Dryden and Dolores is Ms. Dickson.

Daria Dedham taught Spanish at Kennedy.
Delia Dryden taught history at Roosevelt.
Diana Dunn taught science at Coolidge.
Dolores Dickson taught literature at Polk.

SUSPECT GROUP 3

The history teacher's last name wasn't Hall or Harris (#2) or Hubbard (#3), so it was Hayes, and her first name is Hester (#4). Helen's last name isn't Hall or Harris (#2), so it must be Hubbard. Helen Hubbard didn't teach at Roosevelt (#2) or Garfield or Kennedy (#3), so she taught at Coolidge; Harriet also didn't teach at Garfield or Kennedy (#3), so she taught at Roosevelt. Since Hester taught history, she didn't teach at Kennedy (#3), so she taught at Garfield and Hilda taught at Kennedy. The literature teacher wasn't Hester (who taught history), Harriet (#3), or Hilda (#4), so she was Helen. Harriet didn't teach Spanish (#3), so she taught math and Hilda taught Spanish. Since Harriet taught at Roosevelt, her last name is Hall (#2), and Hilda's is Harris.

Harriet Hall taught math at Roosevelt.
Helen Hubbard taught literature at Coolidge.
Hester Hayes taught history at Garfield.
Hilda Harris taught Spanish at Kennedy.

SUSPECT GROUP 4

Ms. Johnston taught at Garfield (#6). Since Ms. Johnston didn't teach literature (#5), the literature teacher wasn't at Garfield; she also didn't teach at Coolidge (#3) or Kennedy (#5), and since the science teacher was at Polk (#6), the literature teacher taught at Roosevelt; her first name was Joan (#4). Her last name isn't Jeffries (#5), so it's James, and Ms. Jeffries taught at Kennedy (#5). Since Ms. Jordan didn't teach at Roosevelt, she taught at Polk (#2), and Ms. Jenkins taught at Coolidge. Since Ms. Jordan taught science, Ms. Jenkins taught Spanish and Ms. Jordan is Jill (#2). Jessica taught math (#4); since she's not Ms. Jeffries (#5), she's Ms. Johnston. Jacqueline isn't Ms. Jenkins (#2), so she's Ms. Jeffries, and Julie is Ms. Jenkins.

Jacqueline Jeffries taught history at Kennedy.
Jessica Johnston taught math at Garfield.
Jill Jordan taught science at Polk.
Joan James taught literature at Roosevelt.
Julie Jenkins taught Spanish at Coolidge.

SUSPECT GROUP 5

Mr. Richards taught at Polk (#4). The teacher at Garfield wasn't Richards, Redding (#7), or Ruiz (#2), and since his name was Ralph or Ryan (#7), he wasn't Roberts (#3); thus, he was Mr. Randall, who taught math (#5). Mr. Roberts didn't teach at Coolidge or Roosevelt (#3), so he taught literature at Kennedy (#6). Since Mr. Randall taught at Garfield, his name is Ralph or Ryan (#7); it is not Ralph (#5), so it is Ryan. Mr. Redding, then, is named Ralph (#7). He didn't teach at Roosevelt (#3), so he taught at Coolidge and Mr. Ruiz taught at Roosevelt. Ralph Redding didn't teach history (#3) or science (#5), so he taught Spanish. Reggie didn't teach literature (#3) or science (#8), so he taught history. He didn't teach it at Roosevelt (#3), so he taught at Polk, and the science class was at Roosevelt. Roland's last name isn't Ruiz (#2), so it's Roberts, and Ray is Mr. Ruiz.

Ralph Redding taught Spanish at Coolidge.
Ray Ruiz taught science at Roosevelt.
Reggie Richards taught history at Polk.
Roland Roberts taught literature at Kennedy.
Ryan Randall taught math at Garfield.

CRACKING THE CASE OF THE SUBSTANDARD SUBSTITUTE

Consider the two teachers that taught the same subject mentioned in #2. Bradley must be the Polk teacher, and the only subjects repeated among the other teachers are Spanish and literature. Suppose the two teachers taught Spanish; then they are Harris and Jenkins, and they went out with (in some order) Bradley and Roberts (the only other teacher who taught at Kennedy). This leaves Dryden, James, and Ruiz, all of whom taught at Roosevelt; two of them must have gone out together, but this is impossible (#1). Therefore, the two teachers in #2 taught literature and are James and Roberts. They went out with Bradley and Harris; since Harris and Roberts both taught at Kennedy, they did not go out together (#1), so James went with Harris and Roberts went with Bradley. This leaves Dryden, Jenkins, and Ruiz. Ruiz didn't go out alone (#3) and didn't go out with Dryden (#1), so he went with Jenkins, and Dryden is left unaccompanied.

Bert Bradley went out with Roland Roberts.
Hilda Harris went out with Joan James.
Julie Jenkins went out with Ray Ruiz.
Delia Dryden is the Phantom.

THE CASE OF THE TRUE LEBLEU

AUCTION WEEK 1

The $1000 painting was sold at Clarissa's (#1). Since the $2000 and $3000 paintings weren't sold at Beverly's or Eloise's (#3), they were sold at Agatha's and Darlene's, and $4000 and $5000 paintings were sold at Beverly's and Eloise's. If the Agatha's painting were $3000, Mr. Black's painting would be $4000; since Mr. Brown's painting was $4000 (#4), Mr. Black's painting must have cost $5000 and the Agatha's painting $2000 (#2), leaving the $3000 painting to Darlene's. Mr. Green's painting didn't cost $2000 or $3000 (#3), so it was $1000. Mr. Gold's painting cost $2000 or $3000 and the painting from Eloise's cost $4000 or $5000; the only way for their sum to have been a multiple of $3000 (#5) is if Mr. Gold's painting was $2000 and the painting sold at Eloise's was $4000; this leaves $3000 as the cost of Mr. White's painting, and $5000 as the cost of the painting sold at Beverly's.

Agatha's sold to Mr. Gold for $2000.
Beverly's sold to Mr. Black for $5000.
Clarissa's sold to Mr. Green for $1000.
Darlene's sold to Mr. White for $3000.
Eloise's sold to Mr. Brown for $4000.

AUCTION WEEK 2

The $5000 painting wasn't sold at Clarissa's (#1), Agatha's (#2), Eloise's (#3), or Beverly's (#4), so it was sold at Darlene's, and Mr. Black spent $2000 (#2). This means Mr. Green, who spent twice as much as the Beverly's buyer (#4), must have spent $4000, and the Beverly's painting sold for $2000. The $4000 painting wasn't sold at Agatha's (#2) or Clarissa's (#1), so it was sold at Eloise's. The $5000 painting was thus not sold to Mr. White (#3), and it wasn't sold to Mr. Gold (#2), so it went to Mr. Brown. That means the buyer at Clarissa's spent $3000 (#1) and the Agatha's painting cost $1000. Mr. Gold must have spent $3000 (#2), and Mr. White spent $1000.

Agatha's sold to Mr. White for $1000.
Beverly's sold to Mr. Black for $2000.
Clarissa's sold to Mr. Gold for $3000.
Darlene's sold to Mr. Brown for $5000.
Eloise's sold to Mr. Green for $4000.

AUCTION WEEK 3

There are only two ways in which two paintings can add up to exactly $4000 more than the sum of two other paintings as described in #4: Case 1, $3000 and $4000 compared to $1000 and $2000, or Case 2, $4000 and $5000 compared to $2000 and $3000. This means (#4) that neither Mr. Green nor Mr. Black bought a painting for $1000 or $2000, and one of them spent $4000. Since Mr. Brown also didn't spend $1000 or $2000 (#3), those costs were for Mr. Gold's and Mr. White's paintings. Suppose Case 1 is true. In this scenario, Mr. Brown bought the $5000 painting, so the Agatha's painting was at most $4000 (#3) and Mr. Gold's painting was at most $2000. In order to satisfy #1, the Agatha's painting must have been $4000 and Mr. Gold's painting $2000. This means that Mr. White's painting cost $1000. But if Mr. White spent $1000 and Mr. Brown spent $5000, the painting from Darlene's must have cost $4000 (#3), which is a contradiction.

Therefore, Case 2 is true, so Mr. Brown spent $3000. This means (#3) that the painting at Darlene's and Mr. White's painting were $1000 and $2000; since the $2000 painting was sold at either Beverly's or Clarissa's, it was sold to Mr. White, and the $1000 painting was sold at Darlene's to Mr. Gold. Since Mr. Gold spent $1000, the painting at Agatha's was sold for $5000 (#1), and the $4000 painting was sold at Eloise's. The Beverly's painting was $3000 less than a painting bought by someone other than Mr. Green (#2), so it must have cost $2000 and the Clarissa's painting cost $3000; subsequently, Mr. Green did not buy the $5000 painting, so he bought the $4000 painting and Mr. Black bought the $5000 painting.

Agatha's sold to Mr. Black for $5000.
Beverly's sold to Mr. White for $2000.
Clarissa's sold to Mr. Brown for $3000.
Darlene's sold to Mr. Gold for $1000.
Eloise's sold to Mr. Green for $4000.

AUCTION WEEK 4

The seascape was sold at Eloise's and cost either $2000 or $4000 (#5). The painting from Agatha's was the portrait (#3), and since it was $2000 less than Mr. Green's but $1000 more than the painting from Clarissa's, it cost either $2000 or $3000; this means the $2000 painting was from either Agatha's or Clarissa's, so the painting from Eloise's was $4000 and Mr. Brown bought the mural for $2000 (#5). This means the portrait from Agatha's must have cost $3000, the Clarissa's painting $2000, and Mr. Green's painting $5000 (#3).

The $5000 painting wasn't sold at Beverly's (#2), so it was from Darlene's, and the $1000 painting was sold at Beverly's. This means Mr. Gold's painting cost $4000. The Darlene's painting wasn't the still life (#4), so it was the landscape, and the Beverly's painting was the still life. Finally, Mr. White didn't buy the still life (#4), so he bought the portrait and Mr. Black bought the still life.

Agatha's sold the portrait to Mr. White for $3000.
Beverly's sold the still life to Mr. Black for $1000.
Clarissa's sold the mural to Mr. Brown for $2000.
Darlene's sold the landscape to Mr. Green for $5000.
Eloise's sold the seascape to Mr. Gold for $4000.

AUCTION WEEK 5

The portrait cost $4000 (#6). The $1000 painting wasn't the landscape (#2), seascape (#3), or still life (#2), so it was the mural. The $2000 painting wasn't the landscape (#2) or seascape (#3), so it was the still life. Then the painting from Eloise's must have cost $1000 (#2). Since Mr. Green's painting wasn't from Eloise's (#7), it wasn't $1000. It was less than $4000 (#4) and wasn't $3000 (#7), so it cost $2000, and the Beverly's painting cost $4000 (#4). Since the painting from Darlene's didn't cost $5000

(#3), it was at most $3000, so Mr. Gold's painting must have cost $1000 (#3) and came from Eloise's.

The paintings from Beverly's and Clarissa's weren't sold to Mr. Black or Mr. White (#5), and the painting from Beverly's wasn't sold to Mr. Green (#4), so Mr. Green bought his painting at Clarissa's, and Mr. Brown bought his at Beverly's. Since the seascape was more expensive than the painting from Darlene's (#3), the seascape cost $5000 and was bought at Agatha's, and the landscape cost $3000 and was bought at Darlene's. Since Mr. Black didn't buy the seascape (#5), he bought the landscape and Mr. White bought the seascape.

Agatha's sold the seascape to Mr. White for $5000.
Beverly's sold the portrait to Mr. Brown for $4000.
Clarissa's sold the still life to Mr. Green for $2000.
Darlene's sold the landscape to Mr. Black for $3000.
Eloise's sold the mural to Mr. Gold for $1000.

CRACKING THE CASE OF THE TRUE LEBLEU

Eloise's is the only auction house that sold four paintings at the same price, $4000; the other was sold for $1000 to Mr. Gold, so he is Puce or Turquoise (#2). Mr. Gold bought from four auction houses, so he is not Puce (#1); thus, he is Turquoise. The total amounts paid were $11000 (Mr. Gold), $14000 (Mr. White), $16000 (Mr. Black and Mr. Green), and $18000 (Mr. Brown). Mr. Brown isn't Vermilion (#1), so Vermilion is either Mr. Black or Mr. Green, and Umber is Mr. White. Mr. Brown is also not Puce (#1), so he is Chartreuse. The only amount Umber never spent is $4000, so Vermilion isn't Mr. Black, who also never spent $4000 (#3). Thus Vermilion is Mr. Green, and Puce is Mr. Black. The two buyers who ended up with the same two genres of paintings are Mr. Black and Mr. Green, who bought a landscape and a still life. There were three occasions on which someone bought a painting for half the total price Mr. Black and Mr. Green paid: Mr. White in Week 1, Mr. Gold in Week 2, and Mr. White in Week 4. One of these was the stolen painting (#4). Mr. White is the buyer who spent $1000 more than Chartreuse twice, so he did not buy the stolen painting (#5); thus Mr. Gold did in Week 2.

Mr. Black is William Puce.
Mr. Brown is David Chartreuse.
Mr. Gold is John Turquoise, who bought the stolen painting from Clarissa's in Week 2.
Mr. Green is Arthur Vermilion.
Mr. White is Richard Umber.

The Case of the Unknown Calzone

LUNCH 1

Table 2 had sausage (#4), so the ingredient shared by tables 3 and 4 (#2) wasn't sausage. Nor was it onions (#4) or meatballs (#2), so it was peppers. Since every ingredient occurred twice, and every ingredient occurred once on tables 1 and 3 (#3), every ingredient occurred once on tables 2 and 4. Since table 4 didn't have onions (#4), table 2 did, and table 4 had meatballs. Since tables 3 and 4 had different ingredients, table 3 didn't have meatballs, so table 1 did. Since tables 2 and 3 didn't share onions (#2), table 3 had sausage and table 1 had onions.

Table 1: meatballs, onions
Table 2: onions, sausage
Table 3: peppers, sausage
Table 4: meatballs, peppers

LUNCH 2

Table 5 didn't have chicken or ham (#2), and since both table 1 and either table 2 or 4 had basil (#3), table 5 had sausage and pepperoni. The ingredient table 3 and table 5 shared wasn't pepperoni (#4), so it must have been sausage. Since table 5 and either table 2 or 4 had pepperoni (#3), table 1 didn't. It also didn't have ham (#5), so it had chicken. Since tables 1 and 5 didn't have ham and tables 2 and 4 had no ingredients in common (#3), table 3 had ham. The ingredient tables 2 and 3 had in common (#4) wasn't sausage, so it was ham. Table 2 can't have had basil (#5), so table 4 did. If table 4 had chicken it would have had the same ingredients as table 1; therefore, table 2 had chicken and table 4 had pepperoni.

Table 1: basil, chicken
Table 2: chicken, ham
Table 3: ham, sausage
Table 4: basil, pepperoni
Table 5: pepperoni, sausage

LUNCH 3

Table 1 had spinach (#4), table 2 had ham (#3), and table 6 had chicken (#3). Since tables 1, 4, and 5 had all six ingredients (#6), so did tables 2, 3, and 6; that means tables 2 and 3 didn't have chicken, so table 5 did (#5). Since tables 3 and 6 didn't have peppers (#4), table 2 did. The ingredient tables 3 and 5 had in common wasn't bacon (#2), and chicken, ham, peppers, and spinach were all served at other tables, so these two tables both

had meatballs. This means table 5 didn't have ham, and neither did table 4 (#4), so table 1 did (#6), and so table 4 had bacon and peppers. That means table 3 didn't have bacon (#2), so table 6 did, and table 3 had spinach.

Table 1: ham, spinach
Table 2: ham, peppers
Table 3: meatballs, spinach
Table 4: bacon, peppers
Table 5: chicken, meatballs
Table 6: bacon, chicken

LUNCH 4

Table 1 had basil (#6), table 2 had peppers (#4), table 3 had sausage (#2), table 4 had onions (#2), and table 5 had chicken (#4). Since tables 1 and 4 have exactly one ingredient in common (#3), every ingredient was served at at least one of these two tables. Since table 1 didn't have sausage (#6), table 4 did. Since only one table had both chicken and basil (#5), every table had at least one of these two ingredients, so table 4 did not have peppers and table 1 did, by the argument above. That means the table that had sausage and peppers wasn't table 1 or 4, so it was table 5 (#5). Table 2 didn't have sausage, so the two ingredients it shared with table 5 were chicken and peppers. Suppose for a moment that table 1 didn't order onions. Then tables 2 and 3 did; table 2 then did not have basil, so tables 3 and 4 did. But this would mean tables 3 and 4 had the same three ingredients. Therefore, table 1 did have onions. Since tables 1 and 4 had onions in common, table 4 didn't have basil (#3) and instead had chicken, and so tables 2 and 3 had basil. The remaining ingredient at table 1 must have been peppers, and the last ingredient at table 3 was onions.

Table 1: basil, onions, peppers
Table 2: basil, chicken, peppers
Table 3: basil, onions, sausage
Table 4: chicken, onions, sausage
Table 5: chicken, peppers, sausage

LUNCH 5

Table 1 had bacon (#5), table 2 had meatballs (#5), and table 3 had basil (#3). Since tables 1 and 5 had no ingredients in common (#2), every ingredient appeared in exactly one of them. So table 5 did not have bacon, and since table 5 did not have pepperoni (#5), table 1 did. Since tables 2, 3, 4, and 6 feature each ingredient exactly twice, and tables 4 and 6 have two ingredients in common, tables 2 and 3 also have two ingredients in common. These ingredients were not basil (#5), meatballs (#3), spinach (#3), or onions (#4), so they were bacon and pepperoni. This means tables 2 and 3 didn't have onions, and since only two of tables 4, 5, and 6 did (#4), table 1 did as well. Since tables 1, 2, and 3 didn't have spinach, the other three tables did. Table 5 had all the ingredients table 1 didn't, so it also had basil and meatballs, meaning tables 4 and 6 had onions. Finally, since tables 2 and 6 had at least one ingredient in common (#2), there were meatballs at table 6 and basil at table 4.

Table 1: bacon, onions, pepperoni
Table 2: bacon, meatballs, pepperoni
Table 3: bacon, basil, pepperoni
Table 4: basil, onions, spinach
Table 5: basil, meatballs, spinach
Table 6: meatballs, onions, spinach

CRACKING THE CASE OF THE UNKNOWN CALZONE

Since two consecutive two-digit calzones contained a 3 (#2), the 3 ingredient must have been repeated at lunches 1 and 2 or at lunches 2 and 3, which only describes sausage, chicken, or ham. Furthermore, the other digit of each of these calzones is in 568, so both were served at lunch 4 (#3). This is impossible for sausage at lunch 2 and for chicken at lunch 3, so ham must mean 3. Since 53 was served at lunch 3 and ingredient 5 was served at lunch 4, peppers mean 5. Either chicken or sausage means 6. Suppose that sausage means 6. Then the 568 calzone at lunch 4 had sausage and peppers, so chicken must mean 8. But chicken wasn't served at lunch 5, and the 8 ingredient was (#3), so this is impossible. Therefore, chicken means 6.

The 568 calzone at lunch 4 had chicken and peppers, so the third ingredient was either sausage or basil; we have already noted that the 8 ingredient can't be sausage, so it's basil. So the other two ingredients in the 801 calzone at lunch 5 were either bacon/pepperoni, onions/spinach, or meatballs/spinach. Since there was a 12 calzone at lunch 3 (#5), the 1 ingredient was served at lunch 3, where it was paired with the 2 ingredient. Onions and pepperoni weren't served at lunch 3, bacon was paired only with ingredients already assigned to digits, and meatballs and spinach were paired only with either ingredients already assigned to digits or each other. Therefore the meatballs/spinach calzone must be the 12 calzone; so onions mean 0, spinach means 1, and meatballs mean 2.

This leaves bacon, pepperoni, and sausage for 4, 7, and 9. Of these, the only two that were ever paired in a two-ingredient calzone were pepperoni and sausage; so this must have been the 47 calzone (#4) and bacon means

9. Since there was a basil/pepperoni calzone served, pepperoni can't mean 4 (#4), so pepperoni means 7, and sausage means 4.

0 = onions
1 = spinach
2 = meatballs
3 = ham
4 = sausage
5 = peppers
6 = chicken
7 = pepperoni
8 = basil
9 = bacon

So where's Sure Locke? His calzone (#6) translates to 19043; this is, appropriately enough, the ZIP code for Holmes, Pennsylvania.

THE CASE OF THE SINFUL CINEPHILES

MONDAY NIGHT

Suppose that Valerie did not attend the midnight showing. Then Steve did not attend at 9 P.M. (#3), so he attended at 6 P.M. and midnight (#4). This means Ursula attended at midnight (#2). Since there are only three different ways for someone to attend two showings, and no one attended all three, Ursula did not attend at 6 P.M. or 9 P.M. (#4). But this means Trixie didn't attend at 9 P.M. (#1), and so Trixie must have attended the same two showings as Steve (#4), which is impossible. Therefore, Valerie did attend at midnight, and so Steve did not (#5). Steve attended at 6 P.M. and 9 P.M. (#4), and so Ursula attended at midnight. By the same argument used above, Ursula did not attend at 6 P.M. or 9 P.M., so Trixie did not attend at 9 P.M. (#1). This means she did attend the other two showings (#4), and since Valerie's two showings (#4) were different from Steve's and from Trixie's, they were at 9 P.M. and midnight.

Steve attended showings at 6 P.M. and 9 P.M.
Trixie attended showings at 6 P.M. and midnight.
Ursula attended a showing at midnight.
Valerie attended showings at 9 P.M. and midnight.

TUESDAY NIGHT

Xavier attended the 6 P.M. showing, and Walter attended at midnight (#1). Suppose that Ziggy did not attend the 6 P.M. showing. Then Xavier attended at midnight (#3), so he attended at least two showings; this is impossible, since Ziggy would have attended at most two (#5). Therefore, Ziggy did attend at 6 P.M. If Walter and Yvette both attended at 9 P.M., Xavier and Yvette would both have missed the midnight showing (#2, #3), which would make it impossible for more suspects to have attended at midnight than 6 P.M. (#4). Therefore, one of them did not attend at 9 P.M., and both Xavier and Ziggy did (#4). Since one of Xavier and Yvette missed the midnight showing (#2, #3), and at least two suspects attended at 6 P.M., two attended at 6 P.M. and three attended at midnight (#4). That means Walter and Yvette missed the 6 P.M. showing, and Ziggy attended at midnight. Since Xavier and Ziggy didn't attend the same set of showings, Xavier did not attend at midnight, and so Yvette attended at 9 P.M. (#3). This means Walter did not attend at 9 P.M. (#4), and so Yvette attended at midnight (#2).

Walter attended a showing at midnight.
Xavier attended showings at 6 P.M. and 9 P.M.
Yvette attended showings at 9 P.M. and midnight.
Ziggy attended showings at 6 P.M., 9 P.M., and midnight.

WEDNESDAY NIGHT
Steve did not attend at 9 P.M. (#3), Walter attended at 6 P.M. (#4), and Ziggy attended at midnight (#4). Walter did not attend at 9 P.M. (#5). Since Valerie did not attend both the 6 P.M. and 9 P.M. showings (#5), she attended at most two showings; since she attended more than Ziggy (#2), Ziggy only attended at midnight, and Valerie also attended at midnight, along with one other showing. At least two suspects attended at 9 P.M. (#3); they must have been Valerie and Yvette, so these two did not attend at 6 P.M. (#5). Steve must also have attended at 6 P.M., since at least two suspects did (#3). If Walter and Yvette both attended the midnight showing, there would have been at least four suspects at that showing. Since this didn't happen (#3), neither of them attended at midnight (#1). Finally, since Steve and Walter didn't attend the same combination of showings, Steve attended at midnight.

Steve attended showings at 6 P.M. and midnight.
Valerie attended showings at 9 P.M. and midnight.
Walter attended a showing at 6 P.M.
Yvette attended a showing at 9 P.M.
Ziggy attended a showing at midnight.

THURSDAY NIGHT
The total number of showings attended by Steve and Ursula was the same as the total number of attendances at 6 P.M. and midnight (#3, #5). Any attendance at 6 P.M. or midnight by Steve or Ursula counts toward one of their total attendances, so if anyone besides Steve or Ursula attended at 6 P.M. or midnight, Steve or Ursula must have attended at 9 P.M. to account for it in their combined total. Since Walter attended at midnight (#6), and either Trixie or Xavier attended at 6 P.M. (#1), Steve and Ursula both attended at 9 P.M.; Trixie and Xavier did not attend at midnight; and Walter, along with one of Trixie and Xavier, did not attend at 6 P.M.

No one attended all three showings or missed all three showings (#2), and in addition, based on information determined so far, no one attended only the 6 P.M. and midnight showings. There are only five other combinations, so each occurred once. The only suspect that could have attended only the midnight showing was Walter. Since Walter didn't attend at 9 P.M., neither did Trixie (#1). Since Trixie didn't miss all three showings, she attended at 6 P.M., and Xavier did not. Since Xavier didn't miss all three showings, he attended at 9 P.M., and thus Ursula attended at 6 P.M. (#4). Since Ursula didn't attend all three shows, she missed the midnight showing, and as the last possible combination, Steve attended at 9 P.M. and midnight, but not at 6 P.M.

Steve attended showings at 9 P.M. and midnight.
Trixie attended a showing at 6 P.M.
Ursula attended showings at 6 P.M. and 9 P.M.
Walter attended a showing at midnight.
Xavier attended a showing at 9 P.M.

FRIDAY NIGHT
There are eight possible combinations of attendances; two of these, attending only at midnight and attending only at 6 P.M. and midnight, violate Clue #3, so every other combination occurred once. In particular, exactly three of these combinations involve attending at 6 P.M. Yvette attended at 6 P.M. (#5), as did two of Trixie, Ursula, and Ziggy (#7), so Valerie and Xavier did not. Therefore, Ursula didn't attend at 9 P.M. (#2), and Ziggy did not attend at midnight (#1). Since Ziggy attended at most two showings and Trixie attended at least one, Trixie attended only at 9 P.M. and Ziggy attended both at 6 P.M. and 9 P.M. (#4). Ursula must have attended at 6 P.M. (#7), and since she didn't attend at 9 P.M., she didn't attend at midnight (#3). The only unused attendance combination that includes the 6 P.M. showing is attending all three showings, so Yvette attended all three. Valerie attended at midnight (#6), so she also attended at 9 P.M. (#3). The remaining combination is missing all three showings, so Xavier missed all three.

Trixie attended a showing at 9 P.M.
Ursula attended a showing at 6 P.M.
Valerie attended showings at 9 P.M. and midnight.
Xavier attended no showings.
Yvette attended showings at 6 P.M., 9 P.M., and midnight.
Ziggy attended showings at 6 P.M. and 9 P.M.

CRACKING THE CASE OF THE SINFUL CINEPHILES

Walter and Xavier attended three showings, Trixie and Ursula attended four, and the other four suspects each attended six. That means the smugglers were one of Walter and Xavier, one of Trixie and Ursula, and two of the others (#1). Xavier wasn't a smuggler (#2), so Walter was. Since Walter was a smuggler, Trixie wasn't (#4), so Ursula was. Of the other four, Valerie wasn't a smuggler (#2), and exactly one of Yvette and Ziggy was (#3), so Steve was as well. Finally, none of Steve, Ursula, and Walter ever saw only the 9 P.M. showing on a night; since the other smuggler did (#3), she must be Yvette.

Steve, Ursula, Walter, and Yvette are the smugglers.

THE CASE OF THE ACROBATIC ARCHBANDITS

GYMNASTICS MEET 1

Suppose #4a is true. Then Marcello competed on the rings, so #1b and #3b are false. Thus #1a and #3a are both true, but since they contradict each other, #4a must be false (and #4b true). So Antonio competed on the trampoline. This means that #2a is false, so #2b is true and Fabio competed on the horse. This means #1b is false, so #1a is true and Giacomo competed on the parallel bars. Since Marcello didn't compete on the rings (#4a is false), he competed in the vault and Luigi competed on the rings.

Antonio scored 6 on the trampoline.
Fabio scored 9 on the horse.
Giacomo scored 10 on the parallel bars.
Luigi scored 8 on the rings.
Marcello scored 7 in the vault.

GYMNASTICS MEET 2

Since either #2a or #2b is true, the brother on the trampoline was Luigi, Primo, Fabio, or Giacomo. Thus #1a is false and #1b is true, so Antonio competed in the vault. This means #5b is false, so #5a is true, and Giacomo competed on the parallel bars or in the floor exercise. This

means #2b is false, so #2a is true, and Luigi's and Primo's events were the horse and trampoline. This leaves Fabio and Marcello as possibilities for the rings; thus #3a is true and #3b is false, which means Luigi didn't compete on the horse, so Luigi's event was the trampoline and Primo's the horse. This means #4a is true, so #4b is false. So Fabio's event was the floor exercise, Giacomo's the parallel bars, and Marcello's the rings.

Antonio scored 8 in the vault.
Fabio scored 10 in the floor exercise.
Giacomo scored 9 on the parallel bars.
Luigi scored 6 on the trampoline.
Marcello scored 5 on the rings.
Primo scored 7 on the horse.

GYMNASTICS MEET 3

Suppose that #1b is true and #1a false. Then Primo competed on the horse, Fabio on the trampoline, and Luigi in the floor exercise. #3b is then true, so #3a is false, and Primo scored a 9. But this leaves an 8 and a 10 for Luigi and Fabio (the trampoline competitor). This means #2a and #2b are both true or both false, a contradiction. So #1a is true and #1b false, meaning that Primo's event was the trampoline, Fabio's the floor exercise, and Luigi's the horse. #3b is false, so #3a is true and Primo did not score a 9. If #2a is true, Luigi scored an 8; but then Primo scored a 10, making #2b also true, a contradiction. Therefore, #2a is false and #2b is true. By #2b, Primo scored 10, and since #2a is false, Luigi scored 9, and Fabio scored 8.

Fabio scored 8 in the floor exercise.
Luigi scored 9 on the horse.
Primo scored 10 on the trampoline.

GYMNASTICS MEET 4

Suppose #6b is true. Then Giacomo scored a 10, and since Marcello didn't score a 9, he scored a 7 or 8. But this means both #2a and #2b are false, a contradiction. Thus, #6a is true and #6b is false, so Marcello scored a 9 and Giacomo did not score a 10. This means #3a is false, so #3b is true and Primo didn't score an 8.

Now, if Giacomo scored the 8, that would leave a 7 and 10 for Antonio and Primo; this would make #4a and #4b either both true or both false. This is impossible, so Giacomo didn't score 8 and Antonio did; this leaves a 7 for Giacomo and a 10 for Primo.

Since Marcello scored 9, #2b is true, so #2a is false, and Giacomo didn't score lower than the score on the parallel bars; but Giacomo had the lowest score, so he must have competed on the parallel bars. Since Primo's score was not 7, #5b is false, so by #5a, Marcello competed in the rings. This makes #1b true, so #1a is false, Antonio did compete in the floor exercise, and Primo competed on the horse.

Antonio scored 8 on the floor exercise.
Giacomo scored 7 on the parallel bars.
Marcello scored 9 on the rings.
Primo scored 10 on the horse.

GYMNASTICS MEET 5
Suppose #6b is true. Then the score on the floor exercise was a 9, so #2a is false and #2b is true, so Antonio scored 8. Also #3b is false, so #3a is true and Primo competed on the trampoline. This means #1a is false, so #1b is true and Fabio was on the rings. Since Giacomo was not on the trampoline, #4a is false and #4b is true, meaning the parallel bars score was 10. Antonio didn't score 9 or 10, so his event was the vault. But this means the trampoline score is 6 or 7, so #7a and #7b are both true, a contradiction.

Therefore #6b is false and #6a is true, so Antonio competed on the rings. This makes #1b false, so #1a is true and Primo was on the parallel bars. This makes #3a false, so #3b is true and the floor exercise score was a 7. This makes #2a false, so #2b is true and Antonio scored an 8. If #7a is true and #7b false, the trampoline and vault scores must have been 6 or 7, but this is impossible since the floor exercise score was 7. So #7a is false and #7b is true, which implies that the trampoline and vault scores were 9 and 10, leaving the 6 for the parallel bars. Since the parallel bars score isn't 10, #4b is false, so #4a is true and Giacomo's event was the trampoline. Since Primo scored a 6, #5b is true, so #5a isn't. That means Marcello's score must be higher than Giacomo's; since Giacomo's was 9 or 10, it must have been 9 and Marcello's was 10, in the vault. This leaves the floor exercise for Fabio.

Antonio scored 8 on the rings.
Fabio scored 7 in the floor exercise.
Giacomo scored 9 on the trampoline.
Marcello scored 10 in the vault.
Primo scored 6 on the parallel bars.

CRACKING THE CASE OF THE ACROBATIC ARCHBANDITS
The total scores for Antonio, Fabio, Giacomo, Luigi, Marcello, and Primo were 30, 34, 35, 23, 31, and 33 respectively. Since there are no repeat total scores, #3b is false and #3a is true. The only brother to achieve the same score three times was Antonio, so he is the lookout.

Only one brother (Antonio) competed in four different events, so #4a is false and #4b is true; this means the muscle and inside man are Fabio (floor exercise) and Giacomo (parallel bars).

Since neither Fabio nor Giacomo ever scored below 7, #1a is false and #1b is true. This means the inside man scored 2 more than another brother; since no brother scored a total of 32, the inside man is Giacomo, the driver is Primo, and the muscle is Fabio. This leaves Luigi and Marcello as the mastermind and safecracker. Neither of these brothers had a repeated score, so #2a is false; thus, #2b is true, the safecracker is Marcello, and the mastermind is Luigi.

Antonio is the lookout.
Fabio is the muscle.
Giacomo is the inside man.
Luigi is the mastermind.
Marcello is the safecracker.
Primo is the driver.

THE CASE OF THE SECURITY IMPURITY

MONDAY
Eugene and Norbert had pairs of passwords that shared three letters (#2); the only three such pairs are BEST and STEP, STEP and PIES, and FAWN and WAND. The first two overlap, so one of the two had FAWN and WAND. One of Norbert's passwords had a first letter that appeared in one of Dexter's passwords (#1); neither F nor W appears in any password other than FAWN and WAND, so FAWN and WAND were not Norbert's passwords; thus, they were Eugene's, and STEP was one of Norbert's. Dexter's passwords were from among BORN, CLUB, MIND, PIES, and BEST. One of them had a fourth letter that appears in the other (#4). This must have been either BORN matched with MIND, or CLUB matched with BEST. If Dexter's passwords were CLUB and BEST, PIES must have been Norbert's (#2). This would mean Lloyd's were BORN and MIND, which share an N, yielding a contradiction (#3). So Dexter's passwords were BORN and MIND. Lloyd's passwords shared no letters (#3), so they were CLUB and PIES, and Norbert's were BEST and STEP.

Dexter's passwords were BORN and MIND.
Eugene's passwords were FAWN and WAND.
Lloyd's passwords were CLUB and PIES.
Norbert's passwords were BEST and STEP.

TUESDAY

Norbert's passwords were either CARD and READ, CHAR and GEAR, or CHIP and ROMP (#1). Eugene's passwords both started with C, or they both started with R (#3). Since one of Eugene's passwords has no matching letters with either of Norbert's (#4), Norbert could not have had passwords starting with both C and R; thus, Norbert's passwords were CHAR and GEAR. Eugene's passwords both started with R, which leaves only one password starting with R; since Lloyd's passwords started with the same letter (#3), they must be CARD and CHIP. By elimination, PLUM was one of Dexter's passwords. The second letter of his other password cannot have been U (#2), so RUNT was one of Eugene's passwords. RUNT has no matching letters with CHAR or GEAR, so Eugene's other password had at least one; it cannot have been ROMP, so it was READ, and ROMP was Dexter's other password.

Dexter's passwords were PLUM and ROMP.
Eugene's passwords were READ and RUNT.
Lloyd's passwords were CARD and CHIP.
Norbert's passwords were CHAR and GEAR.

WEDNESDAY

The only pairs of passwords with exactly two matching letters and starting with different letters are CHASE and SPARE, CHEAT and SHORT, and CLOVE and SLICE. Dexter had one of these pairs of passwords (#1, #2), and it was not CLOVE and SLICE, since SLICE contains an I (#2). The only pairs of passwords with exactly two matching letters and ending with different letters are CHASE and CHEAT, SPARE and SHORT, and CHASE and CRUST, so Norbert had one of these pairs of passwords (#1, #3). The first two would eliminate both of the options for Dexter, so Norbert's must have been CHASE and CRUST, and Dexter's were CHEAT and SHORT. Among the remaining four passwords, the only pairs that have exactly two matching letters are SLICE and SPARE, and SLICE and CLOVE, so Eugene had one of these pairs of passwords (#1). This means SMART was one of Lloyd's passwords. CLOVE and SMART share no letters, so Lloyd's other password wasn't CLOVE (#4). Therefore, CLOVE and SLICE were Eugene's passwords, and SPARE was Lloyd's.

Dexter's passwords were CHEAT and SHORT.
Eugene's passwords were CLOVE and SLICE.
Lloyd's passwords were SMART and SPARE.
Norbert's passwords were CHASE and CRUST.

THURSDAY

The only pairs of passwords for which the first letter of one is the fourth letter of the other are FRESH and SCARF, and CLUMP and TRICK, so Lloyd's pair of passwords was one of these (#1). All of the other passwords fall between CLUMP and TRICK alphabetically, so Lloyd's passwords were FRESH and SCARF, and Dexter's were from among CLUMP, DRAIN, and TRICK (#4). Of the remaining six passwords, three have L as their second letter, so each of the remaining employees had one of these (#2). This means CLUMP was one of Dexter's passwords. If TRICK were his other password, the remaining four passwords would be a pair with A as the third letter, and a pair with E as the third letter. This would make it impossible for Eugene's passwords to have a matching third letter without Norbert's passwords also doing so (#3); thus, Dexter's other password was DRAIN. Eugene's passwords were the only remaining pair with a matching third letter (#3): PIERS and PLEAD. This means Norbert's passwords were PLANK and TRICK.

Dexter's passwords were CLUMP and DRAIN.
Eugene's passwords were PIERS and PLEAD.
Lloyd's passwords were FRESH and SCARF.
Norbert's passwords were PLANK and TRICK.

FRIDAY

Since every password contains an R and a T, Norbert's passwords only shared those two letters (#2), so one of them was CAPTOR, the only password lacking an S, and the other was either FRUITS or TRUISM. The only remaining pairs with a matching fifth letter are COURTS and FRUITS, and PRIEST and TRUISM, so one of these pairs was Lloyd's pair of passwords (#1). Note that this means FRUITS and TRUISM were each entered by Norbert or Lloyd. So Eugene's passwords were from among COURTS, MASTER, PRIEST, SECTOR, and STRIPE. SECTOR and STRIPE both start with the latest available letter alphabetically, and no earlier passwords have earlier last letters, so neither can be Eugene's (#3). COURTS and MASTER is also a disallowed pair (#3), so one of Eugene's passwords was PRIEST, and the other was COURTS or MASTER. This means Lloyd's pair was COURTS and FRUITS. Since FRUITS was Lloyd's password, it was not Norbert's, so Norbert's other password was TRUISM, and since COURTS was Lloyd's password, it was not Eugene's, so Eugene's other password was MASTER. This leaves Dexter with SECTOR and STRIPE.

Dexter's passwords were SECTOR and STRIPE.
Eugene's passwords were MASTER and PRIEST.
Lloyd's passwords were COURTS and FRUITS.
Norbert's passwords were CAPTOR and TRUISM.

CRACKING THE CASE OF THE SECURITY IMPURITY

There were only four password pairs entered by employees other than Norbert on consecutive days with the last letter of the first password matching the first letter of the second, all on Thursday and Friday: PIERS and STRIPE, PIERS and SECTOR, CLUMP and PRIEST, and SCARF and FRUITS. One of these pairs consists of two correct passwords (#4). SCARF and FRUITS were entered by Lloyd on consecutive days, so they cannot both be correct (#1). Thus, the correct passwords on Thursday and Friday were entered by Dexter and Eugene. None of these options were entered on the same day as another password with the same last letter by the same employee, nor were any passwords on Monday, so the correct password on Tuesday was GEAR or CHAR, entered by Norbert, and on Wednesday, since it was not SLICE or CLOVE (#6), it was SHORT or CHEAT, entered by Dexter (#5). Since Dexter entered a correct password on Wednesday, he did not on Thursday (#1); therefore Eugene entered PIERS correctly on Thursday, and Dexter, the ringleader, entered STRIPE or SECTOR correctly on Friday. By elimination, Lloyd correctly entered either CLUB or PIES on Monday. Since PIERS was correct, and no two correct passwords shared more than three letters (#2), PIES and STRIPE are both incorrect, and thus CLUB and SECTOR are correct. SHORT shares four letters with SECTOR, so it is incorrect, and CHEAT is correct. Finally, since CLUB and CHEAT both start with C, CHAR is incorrect (#3), and GEAR is correct.

Monday's correct password was CLUB, entered by Lloyd.
Tuesday's correct password was GEAR, entered by Norbert.
Wednesday's correct password was CHEAT, entered by Dexter.
Thursday's correct password was PIERS, entered by Eugene.
Friday's correct password was SECTOR, entered by Dexter, the ringleader.

THE CASE OF THE LOCOMOTIVE LOCO MOTIVE

SUSPECT GROUP 1

Because the Jamaica suspect's train was four hours before Leonard's and not at 12:30 P.M. (#1), it was in the morning, and Leonard's was in the afternoon. This means Mitch went to Jamaica, and Leonard went to Bermuda (#2). The Bahamas suspect wasn't Orville or Karl (#2), so he was Nate. The Key Largo suspect left in the afternoon, and he also left three hours before a train that was not the last carrying a suspect (#4), so the Key Largo suspect left at 12:30 P.M., and the other two afternoon departures were at 3:30 and 4:30. Leonard left four hours after Mitch, who didn't leave at 12:30 (#1), so Leonard left at 3:30, and Mitch left at 11:30. This means the 4:30 suspect came from Aruba. Nate left one hour before another suspect (#3), so his train left at 10:30, an hour before Mitch. This means Karl left at 12:30 (#3), so Orville left at 4:30.

Nate, coming from the Bahamas, was on the 10:30 train.
Mitch, coming from Jamaica, was on the 11:30 train.
Karl, coming from Key Largo, was on the 12:30 train.
Leonard, coming from Bermuda, was on the 3:30 train.
Orville, coming from Aruba, was on the 4:30 train.

SUSPECT GROUP 2

The lawyer with the duffel bag was either Harrison, Simpson, or Johnson (#1). If it were Harrison, he left three hours after Anderson (#1), one hour before Goodson (#1), and five hours before the lawyer with the fanny pack (#4). This would mean Anderson was on the 8:30, Harrison on the 11:30, Goodson on the 12:30, and the lawyer with the fanny pack at 4:30; but this makes Clue #3 impossible, so Harrison did not have the duffel bag. Similarly, if Simpson had the duffel bag, Anderson left three hours before him (#1), Goodson left one hour after Simpson (#1), Johnson an hour after that (#3), and the lawyer with the knapsack, who must have been Harrison, one hour before Simpson (#3). But in this case, no one left five hours after Harrison, so Clue #4 is impossible.

Therefore, Johnson had the duffel bag, which means Anderson left three hours earlier with the knapsack (#1, #3), Simpson left two hours earlier than Johnson (#3), and Goodson left an hour later than Johnson (#1). Either Simpson or Goodson had the fanny pack, so Harrison left either one hour or four hours before Anderson (#4). This means the only lawyer other than Anderson who could have left one hour before the train with the attaché case (#2) is Johnson, so Goodson had the attaché case, and Simpson had the fanny pack. This means Harrison had the rollaboard and left eight hours before Goodson, which must have been at 8:30, determining everyone else's departure times.

Harrison, with a rollaboard, was on the 8:30 train.
Anderson, with a knapsack, was on the 12:30 train.
Simpson, with a fanny pack, was on the 1:30 train.
Johnson, with a duffel bag, was on the 3:30 train.
Goodson, with an attaché case, was on the 4:30 train.

SUSPECT GROUP 3

Since the pirate with the plank left six hours before Captain Nightmare (#3), the two were at 8:30 and 2:30, 9:30 and 3:30, or 10:30 and 4:30. The pirate with the pegleg left at 9:30 (#6), and Captain Fear left at 2:30 (#6), so the pirate with the plank left at 10:30 and Captain Nightmare at 4:30. Since pirates left at 9:30 and 10:30, no pirate left at 8:30 or 11:30 (#1). Captain Shock left an hour before the pirate with the hat and didn't leave at 3:30 (#2); this means he left at 12:30 or 1:30. If he left at 12:30, the pirate-free trains were at 8:30, 11:30, and 3:30, which in this case makes it impossible for Captain Fright to have left three hours before a pirate-free train (#4). So Captain Shock left at 1:30, and Captain Fear had the hat. The only remaining option for Captain Dread to leave two hours before the pirate with the sword (#5) leaves Captain Dread on the 10:30 train and the pirate with the sword at 12:30. This means the trains with no pirates were at 8:30, 11:30, and 3:30, so Captain Fright left at 12:30, and Captain Terror left at 9:30. Since Captain Nightmare didn't have the eyepatch (#3), he had the parrot, and Captain Shock had the eyepatch.

Captain Terror, with a pegleg, was on the 9:30 train.
Captain Dread, with a plank, was on the 10:30 train.
Captain Fright, with a sword, was on the 12:30 train.
Captain Shock, with an eyepatch, was on the 1:30 train.
Captain Fear, with a hat, was on the 2:30 train.
Captain Nightmare, with a parrot, was on the 4:30 train.

SUSPECT GROUP 4

Giggles's event wasn't the baptism or wedding (#1). The retirement party clown's train and the graduation clown's train were consecutive (#3) before the wedding clown's train (#2), so neither of them was Giggles. And since Giggles's train was later than three other clowns' trains (#1), and the bar mitzvah clown's train was earlier than three other clowns' trains (#4), Giggles wasn't the bar mitzvah clown; therefore, his event was the bachelor party. The wedding clown left before Giggles (#1) and the graduation clown left four hours before the wedding clown (#2), so the graduation clown left at least five hours before Giggles. Toodles left four hours before Giggles (#5), so must have left after the graduation clown. Since both the graduation and retirement party clowns and the pair of Toodles and Yukster were each on consecutive trains, and were four different clowns (#3), both the retirement party clown and graduation clown left before Toodles and Yukster, who both left before Giggles. Since the bar mitzvah clown left before Hilarity and Kabonk (#4), he must have been Slappy and left first; Hilarity left second, Kabonk third, the baptism clown fourth, the wedding clown fifth, and Giggles the bachelor party clown last. If Toodles were the wedding clown, Slappy would have left more than four hours before him (#2) and Giggles four hours after (#5), which is impossible. So Toodles was the baptism clown and Yukster the wedding clown. The graduation clown was not the first to leave but left four hours before the wedding clown (#2), and thus three hours before Toodles (#3), and thus seven hours before Giggles (#5); so the graduation clown was Hilarity and left at 9:30, while Slappy left at 8:30, and Kabonk the retirement party clown left at 10:30. Yukster left at 1:30, Toodles at 12:30, and Giggles at 4:30.

Slappy, going to a bar mitzvah, was on the 8:30 train.
Hilarity, going to a graduation, was on the 9:30 train.
Kabonk, going to a retirement party, was on the 10:30 train.
Toodles, going to a baptism, was on the 12:30 train.
Yukster, going to a wedding, was on the 1:30 train.
Giggles, going to a bachelor party, was on the 4:30 train.

SUSPECT GROUP 5

Since seven trains had designers, only two didn't; that means one empty train left two hours after the other empty train (#4), which left two hours after the designer with the green dress (#6). Since Minerva left at 12:30 (#8), the green dress designer didn't leave at 8:30 or 10:30. If she left at 11:30 or 12:30, it would not be possible for the yellow dress designer to have left in the afternoon an hour before Paula (#2). So the green dress designer left at 9:30, and there were no designers on the 11:30 and 1:30 trains. Ilsa left three hours after the red dress designer (#5), so she left after 1:30; the trains three hours before 2:30 and 4:30 had no designers, so Ilsa left at 3:30, and Minerva brought the red dress. Since Paula didn't leave at 3:30, she left at 4:30, and Ilsa brought the yellow dress at 3:30 (#2). Paula's dress wasn't orange or blue (#9), and it wasn't violet (#1), so it was indigo. Since a designer left between the red and blue dress designers (#7), the blue dress wasn't taken at 10:30 or 2:30, so it was on the 8:30 train. The violet dress designer left before the orange dress designer (#1), so they left at 10:30 and 2:30 respectively. Since Kyra and Zelda were on consecutive trains (#3), Kyra didn't take the orange dress at 2:30; therefore, Natasha did, and Kyra took the blue dress at 8:30 (#9). Zelda was then on the 9:30 train (#3), and Vera left at 10:30.

Kyra, with the little blue dress, was on the 8:30 train.
Zelda, with the little green dress, was on the 9:30 train.
Vera, with the little violet dress, was on the 10:30 train.
Minerva, with the little red dress, was on the 12:30 train.
Natasha, with the little orange dress, was on the 2:30 train.
Ilsa, with the little yellow dress, was on the 3:30 train.
Paula, with the little indigo dress, was on the 4:30 train.

CRACKING THE CASE OF THE LOCOMOTIVE LOCO MOTIVE

Clue #1 eliminates the 2:30 train. Clue #2 eliminates the 8:30 train. Clue #3 eliminates the 10:30 train. Clue #4 eliminates the 11:30 train. Clue #5 eliminates the 4:30 train. Clue #6 eliminates the 3:30 train. Clue #7 eliminates the 9:30 train. And Clue #8 eliminates the 12:30 train. This means Railway was on the 1:30 train and was either Simpson, Captain Shock, or Yukster. The lawyer with the attaché case was on the 4:30 train with Orville, so Railway's alias does not contain the letter O; this narrows his identity down to Yukster.

THE CASE OF THE CROOKED CRASHERS

THE FIRST PARTY

Suppose Erin was invited. Then Bret and Drew were as well (#5b). But that means #2b is false, which is a contradiction if Bret is invited. Therefore, Erin crashed. Suppose now that Cora crashed. Then Adam was invited (#3b). Since Bret and Drew weren't both invited (#5b), #2b is true, so Bret was invited and Drew wasn't. But in this case, Cora was the gorilla (#1a), Erin was the devil (#2a), and Bret was not the vampire (#3a), the ghost (#4a), or the cat (#4a). This leaves no costume for Bret. Therefore, Cora must have been invited, and so Adam was not (#3b). Bret was the vampire (#3a), so #4b is false and Drew crashed. This makes #2b true, so Bret was invited. Erin was not the cat or the devil (#1b), and she was not the ghost (#5a), so she was the gorilla. This means the devil was Cora (#2a), and since Adam was not the ghost (#5a), he was the cat and Drew was the ghost.

Adam dressed as a cat and was a crasher.
Bret dressed as a vampire and was invited.
Cora dressed as a devil and was invited.
Drew dressed as a ghost and was a crasher.
Erin dressed as a gorilla and was a crasher.

THE SECOND PARTY

Since #3a, #4a, and #5a account for all of Bret's possible costumes, exactly one of these statements is true, so exactly one of Cora, Drew, and Erin was invited. If Drew were invited, Adam crashed, since #1a contradicts #4b. But in this scenario, Erin crashed, so Cora was dressed as a zombie (#5b), making #1b true, which is a

contradiction. Thus, Drew crashed. If Cora were invited, her costume was either a cat or a police officer (#3b). But again, in this scenario, Erin crashed, so Cora was dressed as a zombie (#5b). So this is also impossible, and Erin must have been invited, while Cora and Drew both crashed. This means Bret was either the gorilla or the police officer (#5a), but he was not the police officer, since he cannot accuse himself of lying (#2a). So Bret was the gorilla. Cora wasn't the cat or the police officer (#3b) or the zombie (#5b), so she was the devil. This makes #1b false, so Adam was crashing. That means Drew wasn't the cat (#1a) or the police officer (#4b), so he was the zombie. Adam wasn't the cat (#5c), so he was the police officer, and Erin was the cat. Since Adam was crashing, #2a is true, and Bret was invited.

Adam dressed as a police officer and was a crasher.
Bret dressed as a gorilla and was invited.
Cora dressed as a devil and was a crasher.
Drew dressed as a zombie and was a crasher.
Erin dressed as a cat and was invited.

THE THIRD PARTY

If Erin crashed, Drew was invited (#5a). This would mean that Erin brought rum or wine (#5b), and that she brought tequila or beer (#4a), which is impossible. So Erin was invited, and Drew crashed. This means the ghost crashed (#4c), so Erin was not the ghost. Therefore, Bret crashed (#2b), and thus Adam was invited (#1c), and so was Cora (#3b). Erin's drink wasn't tequila or beer (#4a) or rum or wine (#5b), so it was soda. Bret's drink was either soda or wine (#2a), so it was wine. Cora's drink wasn't rum or tequila (#3c), so it was beer. And Adam didn't bring tequila (#1b), so he brought rum, and Drew brought tequila. Since Cora brought beer, she was the gorilla (#3a), and since Adam brought rum, he was the police officer (#1a). We already know Erin was not the ghost, and since she brought soda, she was not the vampire (#2c), so she was the zombie. Finally, Bret wasn't the ghost (#5c), so he was the vampire, and Drew was the ghost.

Adam dressed as a police officer, brought rum, and was invited.
Bret dressed as a vampire, brought wine, and was a crasher.
Cora dressed as a gorilla, brought beer, and was invited.
Drew dressed as a ghost, brought tequila, and was a crasher.
Erin dressed as a zombie, brought soda, and was invited.

THE FOURTH PARTY

Statement #5b implies that the total number of crashers was odd, as it was an odd number if Erin were invited, and if she weren't, it was an even number plus Erin. This means #3c is false, so Cora crashed. Since #3b is false, #1b is true, so Adam was invited. This means the odd number of crashers was either one or three. If it were one, Cora would have been the only crasher; in this case Bret was invited but #2b is false, a contradiction. Therefore, there were three crashers and two invitees, so #2b is true and Bret was invited. This means Adam and Bret were the two invitees, so Drew and Erin crashed.

Bret brought tequila (#2a), so Adam brought beer (#4b). Since he brought beer, he dressed as a vampire or zombie (#2c). So the police officer can't have brought beer, which means the police officer brought wine (#3a). That means the zombie didn't bring wine and brought beer (#1a), so Adam is the zombie. Bret wasn't the gorilla (#4a), the police officer (since Bret brought tequila and the police officer brought wine), or the devil (#5a), so he was the vampire, which means Erin was the police officer (#1b). Cora wasn't the gorilla (#4a), so she was the devil and Drew was the gorilla. Drew didn't bring soda (#1c), so he brought rum and Cora brought soda.

Adam dressed as a zombie, brought beer, and was invited.
Bret dressed as a vampire, brought tequila, and was invited.
Cora dressed as a devil, brought soda, and was a crasher.
Drew dressed as a gorilla, brought rum, and was a crasher.
Erin dressed as a police officer, brought wine, and was a crasher.

THE FIFTH PARTY

Since each of the suspects claims to have brought a different beverage (#1a, #2a, #3a, #4a, #5a), it is impossible for there to have been exactly one crasher, since there would be no beverage left for that person except the one they claimed to bring. Therefore, #2c is false, and Bret was a crasher. If #3b is true, both #1a and #5a are false and Adam and Erin were crashers. But if Adam is a crasher, #1c is false and Erin was invited, which is a contradiction, so Cora was a crasher. If Adam were also a crasher, Drew and Erin were both invited, making two invited guests. But then Erin could not truthfully say #5c, so Adam was invited and brought rum (#1a). Of Drew and Erin, at least one was uninvited (#1c). If both were, only one person in total was invited, so #5c is true, which is a contradiction. If Drew were a crasher and Erin were invited, we once again have two invitees in total and Erin could not say #5c, so Drew was invited and brought beer (#4a) and Erin crashed.

Erin was the zombie (#2b). Cora was the cat or the vampire (#4b); since she crashed, she wasn't the cat (#1b), so she was the vampire. Adam wasn't the devil (#3c) or the ghost (#4c), so he was the cat. The devil was not invited (#3c), so Bret was the devil and Drew was the ghost. The devil didn't bring soda (#5b) and neither did Cora (#3a), so Erin did. Bret didn't bring wine (#2a), so he brought tequila, and Cora brought wine.

Adam dressed as a cat, brought rum, and was invited.
Bret dressed as a devil, brought tequila, and was a crasher.
Cora dressed as a vampire, brought wine, and was a crasher.
Drew dressed as a ghost, brought beer, and was invited.
Erin dressed as a zombie, brought soda, and was a crasher.

CRACKING THE CASE OF THE CROOKED CRASHERS

Suppose Cora is innocent. Cora's the only suspect who didn't bring the same beverage twice or wear the same costume twice at the last three parties, so if she's innocent, Bret's statement is true (#2), so he is innocent as well. Cora referred to Adam and Bret (#3), so Adam is also innocent. Adam said there is exactly one thief among Adam, Bret, and Erin (#1), so Erin is a thief. Erin said there is at least one thief among Bret, Cora, and Drew (#5), so Drew must be innocent. But Drew said there is at least one thief among Adam, Bret, and Cora (#4), which is not true, giving a contradiction. Therefore, Cora is a thief, and thus Bret is a thief (#2). This makes #4 and #5 true, so Drew and Erin are innocent, and by #3, Adam is also innocent.

Bret and Cora are the thieves.

THE CASE OF THE SECONDHAND SECOND HANDS

MONDAY

Calvin was on 2nd Avenue (#5) and Biff was not on 7th Avenue (#1). Because Calvin and Biff were ten blocks apart (#1), Biff was on 6th Avenue, and the two were on A and G Street in some order. This means Earl was on 7th Avenue. Dwight was on F Street (#4). Biff, Calvin, and Dwight were the only dealers on A, F, and G Street (#2), and Frank's and Garrett's street was three blocks south of Archie's street (#3), so Archie was on B Street, and Frank and Garrett were on E Street.

This means Earl was at either 7th & C or 7th & D. Since Frank was directly southwest of Earl (#1), he was on either 5th & E or 6th & E. But if he were on 5th Avenue, Garrett was on 2nd Avenue (#2), which is impossible since Garrett's avenue was two blocks east of Archie's (#3). So Frank was at 6th & E, Earl was at 7th & D, Garrett was at 3rd & E, and Archie was at 1st & B. If Calvin were at 2nd & G, Dwight wasn't on 1st, 2nd, or 3rd Avenue (#4), so there would have been no dealer less than three blocks away from him. This wasn't true (#5), so Calvin was at 2nd & A, and Biff was at 6th & G. Dwight must have been on an otherwise unused avenue (#4), so he was on 4th or 5th. If he were on 5th, there would be no single closest dealer, since Biff and Frank were both two blocks away. Since this wasn't true (#4), Dwight was at 4th & F.

Archie was at 1st & B.
Biff was at 6th & G.
Calvin was at 2nd & A.
Dwight was at 4th & F.
Earl was at 7th & D.
Frank was at 6th & E.
Garrett was at 3rd & E.

TUESDAY

The maximum distance of any corner from 4th & E is seven blocks. Calvin and Garrett were at least two blocks from that corner, since Calvin was neither on 4th nor E (#2), so they were two blocks away and Biff was six blocks away (#4). Calvin wasn't on 3rd since either Earl or Garrett was (#1, #2), so Calvin was at 5th & F, and Frank was on A Street (#2), while Garrett was at either 3rd & D or 2nd & E. Biff was not also on A Street (#1), so he was on B Street at either 1st or 7th Avenue.

Calvin is on 5th and Earl and Garrett are on 2nd and 3rd (#2), so no one else is on those avenues (#1). Dwight was also not on 1st or 7th Avenue (#3). If he were on 6th, Archie was on 7th (#3). But neither Biff nor Frank was on 4th (#2), so if neither of them were on 6th or 7th they would both have to be on 1st, a contradiction (#1). Thus, Dwight was on 4th Avenue. Dwight could not have been on E Street (#4) or G Street (#3), and A and B are occupied, so he was on C or D. If he were on D, Archie was at 7th & G (#3), Biff was at 1st & B, Frank was at 6th & A, and Garrett was at 2nd & E, leaving Earl at 3rd & C. But in this scenario, Dwight is not directly northeast of any dealer, which is impossible (#3). Therefore, Dwight was at 4th & C, and Archie was at 6th & E (#3). This means Garrett was at 3rd & D, and Earl was at 2nd & G. Since Frank was at least six blocks away from 6th & E (#3), he was at 1st & A, and Biff was at 7th & B.

Archie was at 6th & E.
Biff was at 7th & B.
Calvin was at 5th & F.
Dwight was at 4th & C.
Earl was at 2nd & G.
Frank was at 1st & A.
Garrett was at 3rd & D.

WEDNESDAY

Based on the communication chain (#1), three pairs of dealers shared three streets, and one dealer (either Calvin or Earl) was alone on his street. Since Calvin was on the same street as Dwight (#5), Earl was the singleton. And since there were an odd number of dealers above D Street (#3), Earl, the singleton, must have been one of these three. Calvin, the seventh dealer, was on 6th or 7th Avenue (#5), so he and Dwight were not north of D Street (#3). The second and third dealers on the chain were also not north of D Street (#3), so the fourth and fifth were. There were only two occupied streets south of C Street, one of which was occupied by Calvin and Dwight, and there were only two occupied streets north of D Street, one of which was occupied only by Earl. Since Frank was northeast of Biff (#2), Frank was north of D Street and Biff was south of C Street. Frank was therefore west of 5th Avenue (#3), so he was on 3rd Avenue (#2). Since the fifth person in the chain was on the same avenue as Dwight, who was on 1st or 2nd (#5), Frank was fourth. Archie and Garrett must have been third and fifth in some order (#6), so Biff was second.

If Biff were on F Street, there'd be no way for Frank to be directly northeast of him (#2) and be both on 3rd Avenue and north of D Street. Therefore, Biff was on D Street (#2), and the dealer between Biff and Frank on the chain was at 3rd & D. Suppose that Biff was at 2nd & D, and Frank was at 3rd & C. Then the third dealer would be only one block away from Biff, so it would have to have been Archie, not Garrett (#4). Dwight and Garrett, the fifth dealer, would have been on 1st Avenue, so Garrett would have been on 1st & C, two blocks away from Biff; this implies that Earl was one block away from Biff (#4) at 2nd & C, but that puts three dealers on C Street, which is impossible (#1). Therefore, Biff was at 1st & D, and Frank was at 3rd & B. This means the fifth dealer must have been at 2nd & B, with Dwight elsewhere on 2nd Avenue. The fifth dealer was three blocks away from Biff, an odd number, so Garrett was the third dealer (#4), Archie was the fifth, and Earl was one block away from Biff at 1st & C. Calvin was on 7th Avenue at either E, F, or G Street; the only one of these positions that was southeast of a dealer other than Archie (#5) was 7th & F, so Calvin was there, and Dwight was at 2nd & F.

Archie was at 2nd & B (fifth in the chain).
Biff was at 1st & D (second in the chain).
Calvin was at 7th & F (seventh in the chain).
Dwight was at 2nd & F (sixth in the chain).
Earl was at 1st & C (first in the chain).
Frank was at 3rd & B (fourth in the chain).
Garrett was at 3rd & D (third in the chain).

THURSDAY

Since Archie was the dealer working on G Street (#8), and Earl and Dwight were eleven blocks apart (#3), they must have been on 1st and 7th Avenue and on A Street and F Street in some order. Since there were two different assistants on F Street and 7th Avenue (#4), Earl and Dwight's corners were, in some order, 1st & F and 7th & A, with assistants Jacques and Patrick. There was a dealer on 2nd & D (#6). Among the remaining streets and avenues, given the relative positions of Frank and Kevin (#5), Frank must have been either at 2nd & D or 3rd & C. Since the dealer on C Street was either Biff or Garrett (#4), Frank was at 2nd & D, and Kevin assisted at 5th & C.

Since Luke didn't work on A Street, B Street (#7), or C Street, and Garrett wasn't on F Street or G Street, Luke was on D Street with Frank, and Garrett was on E Street (#7). That means Garrett was at 4th & E, and Biff was on C Street with Kevin (#4). The only possible corner four blocks away from Luke for Moe (#7) was 3rd & G with Archie, leaving 6th & B for Calvin and Oliver (#6). Nero must have worked at 4th & E with Garrett, so Earl was at 7th & A (#3) and Dwight at 1st & F. Finally, Jacques was not three blocks away from Archie (#8), so he was at 7th & A, and Patrick was at 1st & F.

Archie was at 3rd & G with Moe.
Biff was at 5th & C with Kevin.
Calvin was at 6th & B with Oliver.
Dwight was at 1st & F with Patrick.
Earl was at 7th & A with Jacques.
Frank was at 2nd & D with Luke.
Garrett was at 4th & E with Nero.

FRIDAY

Clues #2 and #5 give the relative positions of three sets of people: Calvin and Moe; Oliver and Biff; and Earl, Jacques, and Garrett. Since Frank worked with Kevin, and Archie worked with Nero (#3), the seven people above stood at five different corners at most, so the list contains at least two dealer-assistant pairs. If Calvin worked with Oliver, Biff and Moe would have been too far apart, and if Biff worked with Moe, Calvin and Oliver would have been too far apart. Thus, the first and third lists must contain a

matched pair, and the second and third lists must contain a matched pair. The only two ways to accomplish this and fit all of the sets into the grid are Case 1: Calvin worked with Jacques and Garrett worked with Oliver, or Case 2: Biff worked with Jacques and Garrett worked with Moe. If Case 2 holds, Earl worked on A Street; Calvin on B Street; Biff, with Jacques, on C Street; Garrett, with Moe, on E Street; and Oliver on G Street. But since Frank was on D Street (#3), this would mean there were dealers on six different streets, which is impossible (#4). So Case 1 holds, meaning Earl was on 1st Avenue; Calvin, with Jacques, on 3rd Avenue; Garrett, with Oliver, on 5th Avenue; Biff on 6th Avenue; and Moe on 7th Avenue.

Earl was five streets further north than Moe, so Earl was on A Street or B Street, and Calvin was on C Street or D Street. Biff and Earl were both four streets further north than Garrett and Oliver (#2, #5), so Biff and Earl were on the same street, which must have been the only street in which multiple corners were occupied (#4). Since Frank and Kevin worked on D Street (#3), Calvin did not. Thus, Earl was at 1st & A, Calvin and Jacques were at 3rd & C, Garrett and Oliver were at 5th & E, Biff was at 6th & A, and Moe was at 7th & F. Archie and Nero must have occupied the third corner on A Street, so they were at 5th & A (#3). Dwight, the only unassigned dealer, was at 7th & F.

Frank & Kevin are the same distance from Patrick's and another dealer's corners; since that other dealer is directly south of yet another dealer, he must be Garrett (#3). There are no corners of equal distance from Garrett's corner and Biff's corner, so Patrick assisted Earl, and Luke assisted Biff. Frank and Kevin were at a corner on D Street the same distance from Earl and Garrett, which was 2nd & D.

Archie was at 5th & A with Nero.
Biff was at 6th & A with Luke.
Calvin was at 3rd & C with Jacques.
Dwight was at 7th & F with Moe.
Earl was at 1st & A with Patrick.
Frank was at 2nd & D with Kevin.
Garrett was at 5th & E with Oliver.

CRACKING THE CASE OF THE SECONDHAND SECOND HANDS

Frank is the dealer referred to in Clue #2, so he will be northwest of either 1st & A, which is clearly impossible, or 6th & E; the only such corner that doesn't violate Clue #1 is 4th & C. Biff is five blocks from 6th & G (#5); the only such corners that don't violate Clue #1 are 3rd & E and 2nd & F. Biff and Frank will be on the same avenues as, in some order, Calvin and Earl (#7). Neither of these two dealers will be on 2nd Avenue (#1), so Biff will be at 3rd & E. Calvin will not be on 3rd (#1), so Calvin will be on 4th directly south of Frank, and Earl will be on 3rd directly north of Biff; the only such corner that doesn't violate Clue #1 is 3rd & B.

Archie and Dwight will be on the same street (#3); that can only be D Street (#1). This means Calvin will not also be on D Street (#4). He will also not be on E Street (#5) or F Street (#1), so he wil be at 4th & G. Archie will be on either 4th Avenue or 7th Avenue (#1), but he cannot be on 4th Avenue with Calvin and Frank (#4), so he will be at 7th & D. Dwight will be on D Street at 3rd, 5th, or 6th Avenue; he cannot be on 3rd (#4) or 6th (#3), so he will be at 5th & D. Finally, one of the dealers will be at 1st & F (#6), and the only dealer remaining for that corner is Garrett.

Archie will be at 7th & D.
Biff will be at 3rd & E.
Calvin will be at 4th & G.
Dwight will be at 5th & D.
Earl will be at 3rd & B.
Frank will be at 4th & C.
Garrett will be at 1st & F.

THE CASE OF THE VAULT ASSAULT

THE ERIE STREET BANK
The fourth, second and fifth digits are, respectively, either 4, 2, and 1, or 8, 4, and 2 (#2). This means that the first and sixth digits are neither 2 nor 4, so they must be 6 and 3 (#4). If the fourth, second, and fifth digits were 4, 2, and 1, the third digit would have to be 3 (#1), which would be a repeated digit; therefore, those digits are 8, 4, and 2, and the third digit is 0 (#1). The sum of the first digits is 10, so two of the digits must be 2 and 5 (#3), meaning that the last digit is 5.

The Erie Street Bank vault combination is 6408235.

THE HURON STREET BANK
The possibilities for the two-digit numbers formed by pairs of adjacent digits that don't start with 0 (#1, #3) are 13, 14, 24, 25, 31, 35, 36, 41, 42, 46, 47, 52, 53, 57, 58, 63, 64, 68, 69, 74, 75, 79, 85, 86, 96, and 97. The only numbers on this list that are exact multiples of other numbers on the list with no shared digits are 52, which is a multiple of 13, and 96, which is a multiple of 24. Thus the combination either starts with 13 and ends with 52, or it starts with 24 and ends with 96 (#3).

If the combination begins with 24 and ends with 96, the fifth digit must be 7, since 6 has been used (#1). The fourth digit must be 5, since 4 and 9 have both been used (#1). The only digits that can be adjacent to both 4 and 5 are 2 and 7 (#1), both of which have been used. Therefore, the combination starts with 13 and ends with 52. The third digit must be 6, since 1 and 5 have been used (#1). The fifth digit is either 7 or 8, since 2 and 3 have been used (#1); there is no digit that can be adjacent to both 6 and 8 (#1), so the fifth digit is 7. The fourth digit is adjacent to 6 and 7, so it is either 4 or 9 (#1). If it is 4, the third through sixth digits are 4, 5, 6, and 7 in a different order, which is impossible (#2). Therefore, the fourth digit is 9.

The Huron Street Bank vault combination is 1369752.

THE MICHIGAN STREET BANK
The third digit is larger than the first, second, fourth, and fifth digits (#1, #2) but two less than the sixth digit (#6), so it is either 4, 5, 6, or 7. Furthermore, the sixth digit is less than, and alphabetically later than, the seventh digit (#3), so the sixth digit cannot be 8 or 9. Therefore, the third and sixth digits are either 4 and 6, or 5 and 7. If the third digit were 4, the first, second, and fourth digits would all be less than 4 and thus have a sum of at most 6, since they are all different. But the sum of these digits is equal to the seventh digit (#4), which is greater than 6 (#3), so this is a contradiction. Thus the third and sixth digits are 5 and 7.

If none of the first five digits were 4, we would have the same contradiction as above, since the maximum sum of the first, second, and fourth digits would be 6. Since the second digit is larger than the first (#1), and the fourth is larger than the fifth (#2), either the second digit or the fourth digit is 4. In either case, the 4 and 5 are a pair of adjacent consecutive digits. This only occurs once (#5), so the seventh digit cannot be 8. Therefore, it is 9 (#3), and so the first, second, and fourth digits are 2, 3, and 4 in some order. The first and second digits also cannot be consecutive (#5), so they are 2 and 4 respectively (#1), and the fourth digit is 3. The fifth digit must be less than 3 and come later in the alphabet (#2); the only unused such digit is 0.

The Michigan Street Bank vault combination is 2453079.

THE ONTARIO STREET BANK
Since there are three disjoint pairs of digits sharing no letters when written (#1, #2, #3), and 2, 4, and 6 are the only digits that do not contain an E when written, each of

the pairs contains one of these digits. The second and fifth digits are odd (#7), and the fourth and seventh digits are even (#5); because of the argument above, the first and sixth digits are each either 2, 4, or 6. Since the first and last digits are both even, the only pair of digits with a sum of 12 must be 4 and 8, and at least one of them is first or last (#6). The seventh digit is an even number that is not 2, 4, or 6. If it were 0, the second digit would be 1 (#5), and since we already know the first digit is 2, 4, or 6, it would have to be 4 (#6); but this is a contradiction, since 4 and 1 both contain the letter O when written (#1). Therefore, the seventh digit is 8, and the second digit is 9 (#5).

The fourth digit, which is even, cannot be 8, which is already used. It cannot be 0, since the fifth digit is one lower (#5). It cannot be 4, since the fifth digit would then be 3 (#5), creating another pair of digits that total 12 (#6). And it cannot be 2, because if it were, the third digit could not be 0 since they share a letter O (#2), and so 2 would be the smallest even number but not adjacent to the 9, a contradiction (#4). Thus, the fourth digit is 6, and the fifth digit is 5 (#5). Since 5 and 4 share an F, the sixth digit is 2 (#3), and the first digit is 4. Since the 2 is not adjacent to the 9, the 2 is not the smallest even number (#4), and so there must be a 0 in the third position.

The Ontario Street Bank vault combination is 4906528.

THE SUPERIOR STREET BANK

The correct combination shares three digits (in the same positions) with an increasing sequence of consecutive digits (#5). Call a digit shared with the sequence "correct." Suppose the sequence is 3456789. The second and fifth digits must both be incorrect since one is three times the other (#1), and the fourth and seventh digits must both be incorrect since one is four times the other (#3). This implies that the third and sixth digits are correct, but 5 and 8 do not differ by 5 (#2), so the sequence is not 3456789.

Suppose the sequence is 2345678. Of the third and sixth digits, if the 4 is correct, the sixth digit is 9 (#2), but the sixth digit isn't the largest (#4). If the 7 is correct, the third digit is 2 (#2), and the first digit is 8 or 9 (#4), which is incorrect, so at least one of each of the other pairs (second and fifth, fourth and seventh) must be correct. But if 2 is already accounted for, the fourth and seventh digits must be 1 and 4 (#3), neither of which can be correct. So neither the third nor sixth digit can be correct. At most one of each of the other pairs can be correct, so the first digit must be a correct 2, but this also leaves 1 and 4 as the only possibilities for the fourth

and seventh digits (#3), meaning once again that neither of them can be correct, so the sequence is not 2345678.

Suppose the sequence is 0123456. The fourth and seventh digits must both be incorrect (#3), one of the third and sixth digits is incorrect (#2), and one of the second and fifth digits is incorrect (#1), so again, one of each of the clue #1 and clue #2 pairs is correct. This implies that the second and fifth digits are 1 and 3 (#1). Since 1 is now used, the fourth and seventh digits must be 2 and 8 in some order (#3). Since 2 is now used, the third and sixth digits must be 0 and 5 (#2). But this implies the first digit is incorrect, which is too many incorrect digits. So the sequence is not 0123456, and by elimination, it must be 1234567.

The seventh digit cannot be correct (#3). The first and fourth digits can't both be correct, because then both the first and seventh digits would be 1 (#3), so at most one of the first, fourth, and seventh digits is correct. One of the third and sixth digits is incorrect (#2), and one of the second and fifth digits is incorrect (#1), so yet again, one of each of the clue #1 and clue #2 pairs is correct. This implies that the second and fifth digits are 2 and 6 (#1), and since 6 is now used, the third and sixth digits are 3 and 8 (#2). Since the first digit is larger than 8 (#4), it must be 9. That means the first digit is incorrect, so the fourth digit must be correct (as noted before), which means the fourth and seventh digits are 4 and 1, respectively.

The Superior Street Bank vault combination is 9234681.

CRACKING THE CASE OF THE VAULT ASSAULT

The second digit of the master combination is one more than the Slip 3 vault's second digit (#3b) and one less than the Slip 1 vault's second digit (#1a). Since the second digits of the vault combinations are 2, 3, 4, and 9, the master combination must have a 3 in the second position, Slip 3 is from the Superior Street vault, and Slip 1 is from either the Erie Street vault or the Michigan Street vault. The sixth digit of the master combination is 7 or 9 (#3a), so the sixth digit for the Slip 4 vault is even (#4a). Thus, Slip 4 is from the Ontario Street vault. This means the fourth digit of the master combination is either 3 or 9 (#4b), and since 3 is used, it's 9. That means the sixth digit is 7.

We've already determined Slip 1 is not from the Huron Street vault, and since the Huron Street vault combination has the same second digit as the master combination, Slip 2 is not from the Huron Street vault (#2b). So Slip 5 is, and the third digit of the master combination is either 5 or 7 (#5a). Since 7 is already used, it's 5. That means the third digit of the Michigan Street combination is correct, so Slip 2 is not from Michigan Street (#2b). That means Slip 2 is from Erie Street, and Slip 1 is from Michigan Street.

In the Michigan Street combination, the third and sixth digits match the master combination, and the second, fourth, and seventh do not. This means either the first or fifth digit is correct, but not both (#1b). Suppose the first digit is correct, and is thus a 2. Then in the Huron Street combination, the second and fourth digits are correct, and all the others are incorrect, a contradiction (#5b). So the fifth digit is correct in the Michigan Street combination, and thus a 0. The second and fourth digits in the Huron Street combination match the master combination, and the third, fifth, and sixth digits do not. So either the first or seventh digit matches, but not both (#5b), meaning either the first digit is a 1, or the seventh is a 2. The seven digits in the master combination add up to 34 (#2a), so the first and seventh digits add up to 10. If the first digit were 1, the seventh digit would have to be 9, which is already used. So the seventh digit is 2, and the first is 8.

The master combination is 8359072.

A DISTURBING LETTER

The letters can be translated as follows:

A = 10 (3 + 9 – 2)
B = 4 (Ursula)
C = 3 (Simpson, Captain Shock, and Yukster)
D = 2 (Bradley and Roberts, Harris and James)
E = 9 (Marcello at the fourth meet and Luigi at the third)
F = 8 (3 + 5 + 0)
G = 4 (the first four)
H = 3 (3rd & E to 1st & F)
I = 6 (A, C, E, R, S, and T)
J = 1 (the second auction only)

The sum of the two smallest primary passcodes is 6 (#10), so they are 1 and 5 or 2 and 4. The only two primary passcodes in which one is twice the other are not the two smallest (#5), so the two smallest primary passcodes are 1 and 5. Since 8 is the smallest passcode which is not both primary and secondary (#7) and 9 is the largest (#6), all other passcodes are both primary and secondary. This means 1 and 5 are also secondary passwords. The smallest and largest secondary passcodes differ by 10 (#2), so 11 is also a primary and secondary passcode, and is the largest of both. The numbers 2, 3, and 4 are not passcodes (since 1 and 5 are the two smallest), but there is a pair of passcodes for which one is double the other (#5), so 10 must also be a primary and secondary passcode. Thus, the passcodes for each category are 1, 5, 8 or 9, 10, and 11. Mac's secondary passcode is a multiple of 3 (#9), so it must be 9, and 8 is a primary passcode.

Since Delta's secondary passcode is one more than four times Giacomo's (#8), Delta's is 5, and Giacomo's is 1. Echo's secondary passcode is one more than Mario's (#11); since Mario's isn't 9, it is 10, and Echo's is 11. Delta and Echo have different secondary passcodes than Mac, Giacomo, and Mario do; Echo is not Charles (#5), so he is Norbert, and Delta is Charles. Echo and Charles have 5 and 10 as their primary passcodes (#5); since Charles has 5 as his secondary passcode, Charles has 10 as his primary (#1), and Echo has 5 as his primary.

The sum of Mario's passcodes is a multiple of 3 (#4), and his secondary passcode is 10, so his primary passcode cannot be 1. Neither can Giacomo's, since his secondary passcode is 1 (#1). Therefore, Mac's primary passcode is 1, and he is Alpha (#5). Bravo's passcodes are 8 or 11 and 1 or 10; their sum is a multiple of 4 (#3), so they must be 11 and 1, making Bravo Giacomo and Charlie Mario.

Alpha is Mac Hacker, with passcodes 1 and 9.
Bravo is Giacomo Ravioli, with passcodes 11 and 1.
Charlie is Mario Desmond, with passcodes 8 and 10.
Delta is Charles McTaggart, with passcodes 10 and 5.
Echo is Norbert Spader, with passcodes 5 and 11.

Extracting letters as described gives the phrase MISTER GOLD. The Boss is auction bidder Mr. Gold, previously identified as John Turquoise.

In the crime-fighting business, some days are easy, and some days you get knocked unconscious and wake up locked in a trunk at the Turquoise estate. Good thing my puzzle-solving associate was able to work out the clues and spring me loose before I polished off the last of the oxygen. But once I emerged, the place was deserted, with no sign of Turquoise or any of his possessions. I called in the boys to dust for prints, but deep down I knew my captor was long gone ... in the real world, criminal masterminds don't roll out the red carpet unless they have an exit strategy. Wherever he was now, it wasn't Enigmaville, so I could set off on a wild-goose chase, or I could calm down and accept that this is one that got away. Thinking about the situation rationally, I let out a long sigh, and headed home.

To pack my bags.